The Violent Society

The Violent Society

By

STUART PALMER

COLLEGE & UNIVERSITY PRESS · *Publishers*
NEW HAVEN, CONN.

TO ANNE AND CATHY

Contents

Ch. IV: The Social Control of Homicide

PART II: INWARD DIRECTED, PERSONAL VIOLENCE: SUICIDE

Ch. V: Theory and Suicide

Ch. VI: Suicide and the Social System

Ch. VII: Suicide, The Individual and Social Control

PART III: MASS VIOLENCE: RACE RIOTS

Ch. VIII: Race Riots, the Social System, and the Individual

Ch. IX: The Social Control of Race Riots

PART I:

OUTWARD DIRECTED, PERSONAL VIOLENCE: HOMICIDE

CHAPTER I

Social Theory and Homicide

1. *Desperation and Aggression*

When individuals feel that they are backed to the wall and that there is no escape, they become violent. Depending upon environmental conditions and their perception of those conditions, individuals aggress against others, against the social system, or against themselves. It is a common mistake in human affairs to think that men feel backed to the wall only when from an objective standpoint they are deprived of what they drastically need. Relative deprivation is as important in the arousal of violence as absolute deprivation and often more so. It is in relation to others that we judge how badly off we are. And frequently we see ourselves as more deprived than objective measures would indicate. When men define themselves as hurt, they become dangerous.

When individuals become violent, social controls are brought into play ostensibly to arrest the violent behavior and to prevent its recurrence. It is not unusual that those controls increase the problem they are manifestly designed to reduce. As a rule, they bring frustration to the violent offender. Thus the offender becomes more aggressive. Unless he is rendered immobile, the tendency of the offender in the face of frustrating controls will be to lash out at the social system and at those individuals who exercise the controls. If he is blocked from doing so, then the offender will turn violently upon himself.

Both before and after social controls come into play, it is in role relationships that individuals feel especially great deprivation. They may be blocked from playing out their roles successfully, they may have roles taken from them, or they may otherwise lose their roles. Stop a person from carrying out his social roles or take those roles from him and you mutilate his humanity.

2. *The Plan of the Book*

These ideas, neither new nor startling, form the basis for the analysis in this study. In this beginning chapter, some remarks on the scope of violence in the United States and elsewhere are made. Violence in general and homicide as a specific form of violence are defined. A number of sociological theoretical formulations of aggressive behavior are reviewed. Common themes among them are specified. A new formulation of homicide emerges, one which focuses on conditions of the social system as they give rise to homicide. In chapter two relevant data are analyzed. Chapter three provides a complementary formulation, which emphasizes certain characteristics of the individual as these are related to homicide. Chapter four is concerned with the social control of homicide.

Part II deals with suicide. The format is much the same as Part I. Theories of suicide are discussed in chapter five and common themes explicated. A formulation of suicide which parallels that of homicide is set forth. Again social system variables are treated first. In chapter six, personality variables are considered. In both instances, data on suicide are brought to bear on the hypotheses that emerge. The social control of suicide is the topic of chapter seven.

One major form of mass violence, racial rioting, is analyzed in chapters eight and nine. Theories of collective behavior are reviewed. A theoretical approach to mass violence is developed, consistent with the formulations of homicide and suicide in earlier chapters. Social system and individual variables are treated, and the social control process as it applies to riots is given considerable attention.

The final chapter draws together the various major ideas which have been pursued throughout the book. New lines of analysis, lines which might profitably be followed in future studies, are delineated. There is no attempt, then, to be encyclopedic. The thrust is on three forms of violence—homicide, suicide, and racial rioting—especially as they obtain in the United States.

3. *Some Dimensions of Violence*

Violence has always been an integral part of human life. And there is little reason to think that life will soon be otherwise. In this century alone, and by conservative estimate, three and a half million homicides and 25 million suicides have been committed around the world.[1] Assault and rape occur in much greater numbers. Revolution and rioting are common.[2] And over the last 60 years the numbers of dead through war, while not known accurately, total in the hundreds of millions.[3]

Since its inception, the United States has been in the front ranks of violent societies.[4] Born in revolution, wracked by civil war, involved in numerous other wars, it has also a tradition of bloody rioting, homicide, and assault.

The latter part of the last century in the United States saw great civil strife as Reconstruction gave way to large-scale racial and labor violence.[5] Mass disorders continue to loom large in the American way of life. One analysis estimates that during a five-year period beginning in 1963, 1100 persons per 100,000 of our population were annually involved in some form of civil strife. Compared with 16 other Western democracies, we rank first in total magnitude of civil strife.[6]

There occur each year in the United States, and these are minimum estimates, 15,000 criminal homicides, 35,000 suicides, 300,000 serious assaults, and 50,000 forcible rapes.[7] Our homicide rate is 30 times that of Ireland, 10 times that of England, and over eight times that of Sweden.[8] While our suicide rates are more nearly the norm for societies around the world than are our homicide rates, we nonetheless exceed many countries in suicide. We have six times as much suicide as Mexico or the Republic of China, over four times as much as Ireland, and more than three times that of Guatemala.[9]

On balance, there are very few signs that our violence is abating. Our concern with the problem is great but our effective control of it is minimal. Activity in the area of prevention of violence is almost nonexistent in the United States. Hardly any attention is given to the rehabilitation of violent offenders.[10]

There is much socially sanctioned retaliation against those who behave violently. And little attempt is made to get at the root causes of violence.

4. Defining Violence and Homicide

Violence may be directed toward others or the self. It may involve physical or psychological frustration. And it must be other than accidental. Violence is, then, severe frustration, physical or psychological, or death inflicted by one or more individuals upon others or themselves that is not accidental.

There are several problems with this definition. They revolve around the ideas of accident, intent, and goal. It is exceedingly difficult in some instances to determine what constitutes accident. When behavior is not accidental, it may involve unconscious motivation rather than conscious intent. Further, if frustration is inflicted by intent, there is the question of whether or not the goal is one that implies violence. For example, if under emergency conditions in the field a physician performs an operation without an anesthetic on a wounded person, this is hardly violence. One can caution only that care be exercised in construing which events are not violent and which are violent in what degree.

As for criminal homicide, one form of violence, societies around the world differ somewhat in their views of what constitutes such behavior. Yet there is a large area of agreement.[11] The vast majority of societies consider the killing of one individual by another that is not accidental, not in the line of culturally prescribed duty and not in self-defense, to be criminal homicide. This is the definition followed here.

In many legal systems, including that of the United States, criminal homicide is classified into four categories on the bases of the degrees of premeditation and "maliciousness" invoved. Granting that it is exceedingly difficult to determine premeditation and maliciousness it will nonetheless be useful to take note of the four types.

Beginning with the most serious these are: first-degree murder, characterized in legal terms by the greatest degree of premeditation and maliciousness. Second-degree murder has lesser degrees of premeditation and maliciousness but more than the third form, non-negligent or first-degree manslaughter. And that in turn is more premeditated and malicious than the fourth and least serious form of criminal homicide, negligent or second-degree manslaughter.

Legal or justifiable homicide should be mentioned. It is not a criminal act. While such homicide involves intent, it is carried out in self-defense or in line of culturally acceptable duty. An example of the latter is the killing by a police office of an escaping arrestee.

5. *Restraints and Social Structuring*

The remainder of this chapter is a review of the major sociological theoretical formulations that either deal directly with or bear significantly upon homicide. The first of these, by Henry and Short, is concerned explicitly with homicide.[12] Henry and Short give major attention to three variables: status, strength of the relational system, and degree of external restraints. By status, Henry and Short mean prestige. By strength of the relational system, they mean the extent to which individuals are involved in social or cathectic relationships with others. By external restraints is meant the degree to which individuals are required to conform to the demands and expectations of other persons.

Henry and Short state, "A person of low status is required to conform to the demands and expectations of persons of higher status merely by virtue of his lower status. A person involved in intense 'social' interaction with another person is required to conform to the demands and expectations imposed as a condition of the relationship. These observations may be summarized in the following proposition: the strength of external restraint to which behavior is subjected varies positively with the strength of the relational system and inversely with position in the status hierarchy."[13]

Henry and Short go on to hypothesize that homicide varies positively with the strength of external restraint over behavior. Low status persons are subjected to one-sided restraints. They must conform to the expectations of those of higher prestige while the latter need not conform to their expectations. This leads individuals of low status to blame others for the frustration they consequently experience. Thus they tend to aggress outwardly toward others rather than toward the self.

Straus and Straus, drawing on their research in Ceylon, suggest an inverse relationship between homicide and the degree to which a society is closely structured.[14] A society is closely structured, Straus and Straus say, to the extent that reciprocal rights and duties are stressed and enforced. Those authors hold that outward violence, homicide in particular, does not tend to be a culturally permissible solution to conflict in a closely structured society. In a society that is loosely structured, homicide is likely to be less impermissible. Why homicide is less impermissible in one type of society than in the other is not fully explained.

Wood takes the position that homicide is closely related to the thwarting of aspirations for upward social mobility.[15] Homicide rates grow high as persons theoretically have opportunity to rise in an invidiously arranged society but are in fact near the bottom and believe they are deprived of upward movement. Here there is a lack of justice, as persons of low prestige see it, for they have on the one hand been afforded the opportunity to raise their status while on the other they are blocked from doing so.[16]

6. Goals, Means, and Opportunities

The works of Cohen[17] and of Cloward and Ohlin[18] are direct descendants of Sutherland's[19] contributions regarding differential association and the criminal subculture. (Sutherland proposed that the greater the association of an individual with others who followed the patterns of the rule- and law-violating criminal subculture, the more likely was that individual to become criminal.) But those works are descendants of the contributions of various others, and in particular of Merton.

In that small classic "Social Structure and Anomie,"[20] Merton took Durkheim's idea of anomie and gave it a form and content it had not previously possessed. In Merton's view, the greater the disparity between cultural goals and institutionalized means for achieving them, the more is a society anomic. When individuals internalize and pursue cultural goals and are blocked from access to relevant institutionalized means, they innovate new means in criminal fashion.

Cohen brings together Merton's formulation and Sutherland's differential association theory. He adds the psychological concept of reaction-formation. Cohen thereby offers an explanation of how the delinquent or criminal subculture develops.[21] His reasoning runs as follows: Lower-class boys in the United States internalize the prevailing cultural goals, which are set by the upper-middle class. But those boys are in large measure denied access to the institutionalized means for achieving the goals. The boys have a reaction-formation to these frustrating circumstances: They behave in ways that are diametrically opposed to the values of the upper-middle class. Thus they lay the groundwork for, and go on to develop the customs, violent and otherwise, that constitute the delinquent subculture. Judged by upper-middle class standards, that subculture is in Cohen's words "non-utilitarian, malicious and negativistic."[22]

Cohen's formulation as so far summarized is not applicable to violence or other delinquency by middle-class boys. In an attempt to explain the latter, Cohen employs a different form of reaction-formation, that of masculine protest. Middle-class mothers are likely to attempt to coerce their sons to be overly good little boys, to force them into a feminine mold. If so, the boys may through reaction-formation go to the opposite extreme: They may assert their masculinity by violence and theft. Their mothers' labeling of them as "good boys" will at least in part be counterbalanced by the wider society's labeling of them as "tough guys."

Cloward and Ohlin's[23] conception of delinquent opportunity structures builds on the formulations of Merton, Sutherland, Shaw and McKay[24] and although with some disagreement, Cohen. Cloward and Ohlin see lack of access to institutionalized means that lead to cultural goals as generating a delinquent subculture. They do not, however, accept Cohen's reaction-formation explanation. Rather they view the emergence of the delinquent subculture as a collective solution to the disparity between means and goals by those who suffer from that disparity.

As Cloward and Ohlin say, "The concept of differential opportunity structures permits us to unite the theory of anomie, which recognizes the concept of differentials in access to legitimate means, and the 'Chicago tradition' (the cultural transmission theories of Shaw and McKay and of Sutherland), in which the concept of differentials in access to illegitimate means is implicit."[25] Depending on lack of access to legitimate means and on illegitimate opportunity, individuals learn to perform roles which are defined by customs within each of three segments of the delinquent subculture: the criminal (theft), the conflict (violence), and the retreatist (notably drug addiction). New members must be accepted by old and socialized to relevant roles. This means that individuals thereby become socially designated, labeled, as thieves, as violent persons, or as retreatists.

7. Subcultures of Violence and Other Approaches

Miller's conception of lower-class culture as one threaded with delinquent and criminal customs is both a cultural-transmission and a conflict approach.[26] The middle class and upper-middle class in particular dominate the society and so set the overall cultural values as to which behaviors are acceptable and which are deviant. Lower-class and middle-class behavior patterns often conflict with each other. The middle-class designates as criminal certain behaviors relatively common to lower class culture, physical violence and theft in particular. Control agents representing the middle-class come into conflict with members of the lower class, label them deviant, and bring to bear against them formal sanctions.

Wolfgang and Ferracuti stress the existence of "subcultures of violence," bodies of custom for the commission of violent acts, as a major explanatory variable.[27] The more integrated with each other are customs for violence, the more does a subculture of violence actually obtain. And the more integrated into that subculture are individuals, the more likely are they to behave violently.[28]

Wolfgang and Ferracuti conclude: "We have not attempted to explain the cause of the subculture of violence. Such an endeavor undoubtedly involves analysis of social class and race relations that would include residential, occupational, and other social forms of discrimination and cultural isolation as important factors. Some consideration of role theory, reference groups, and particularly child-rearing practices that employ physical punishment and promote early overt aggressive patterns would aid the search for causal factors and remedial methods. At this point we are suggesting that further probing analysis of the identified subculture of violence as a meaningful concept in understanding homicide and other assaultive crimes would be most productive if it focused on the creation and description of the value system of this subculture."[29]

Three remaining approaches are especially relevant. The first of these is the "techniques of neutralization" idea of Sykes and Matza.[30] Those authors hold that rather than having a commitment to delinquent or violent subcultures, lower-class youthful violators are in fact committed to middle-class norms. Techniques of neutralization allow those individuals to transgress those norms: To gain middle-class goals, lower-class youths may, if denied legitimate means of access, resort to illegitimate means. Those illegitimate means, violence and theft mainly, run counter to the internalized middle-class norms. In order to reduce the consequent guilt, violators employ a major form of psychological defense: rationalization. Through rationalization they lead themselves to believe that their transgressions are morally justified, that middle-class norms have not been violated with "criminal intent." In this way these boys neutralize what would otherwise be painful feelings of guilt. And they are able to avoid labeling themselves as deviants.[31]

Short and Strodbeck emphasize threats to the status of youthful gang members as precipitants of violence.[32] Threats from within or without the group trigger fights between gangs or occasionally between individuals within a gang. Leaders are especially sensitive to status threats. Leaders may engage in violence with another member of their gang in order to insure their dominance. They may initiate violence toward another gang both to increase their "rep" and to direct outward and away from themselves the aggression of their own gang's members.

Finally, note should be taken of Porterfield's concern with the "well-being" of social entities.[33] His Index of Social Well-Being takes into account various measures of educational, health, and other services in the states of the United States. The level of such social services can be construed as a rough measure of the degree to which individuals help and reciprocate with one another. Porterfield finds that the lower is a state's index of well-being, the higher is the crime rate, including homicide.

8. *Common Themes: Reciprocity and Integration*

The formulations outlined above vary considerably and yet share a number of ideas. Two major common themes are those of reciprocity and social integration. Before considering how these themes run through the approaches discussed above, it will be useful to give some attention to the meanings assigned reciprocity and integration in the wider sociological literature.

Mauss envisioned social interaction as a constant process of giving and receiving—of reciprocity.[34] He stressed the obligation to receive the material gift—which in turn involves the duty to give. "Everything is stuff to be given away and repaid."[35] Homans gives central prominence to "true exchange" in his analysis of the elementary forms of human behavior: "True exchange (is) where the activity of each of at least two animals reinforces (or punishes) the activity of the other, and where accordingly each influences the other."[36] Gouldner views reciprocity as *a pattern of mutually contingent exchanges of gratifications*. Reciprocity is, he suggests, a universal moral norm which contributes to the stability of social systems.[37]

And Coser writes of Marx: "In contrast to the social theorists who cling to a harmony model of society and stress symmetry in the mutual orientation of actors, Marx is concerned with the facts of unilateral dependence and hence of exploitation, and the denial of reciprocity. . . . institutionalized exploitation, the 'right to something for nothing,' to use Veblen's telling phrase, is usually hidden under a veil of claims to the complementarity of the roles of rulers and ruled."[38] In Marxian terms the denial of reciprocity by the bourgeoisie toward the worker led to violent revolution by the latter.

Interaction may be reciprocating to greater or lesser degree. Or it may be unreciprocating in that individuals block one another. While conflict and unreciprocity are similar, the absence of conflict does not necessarily mean reciprocity. Rather, absence of conflict may signify neutrality.[39] Thus the concept of reciprocity (and unreciprocity) has here advantages that conflict does not have.

Durkheim made much use of the idea of social integration, although it is not fully clear precisely what he meant by the term.[40] However, he seems to have meant the degree to which a society or group is characterized by agreement among its members concerning basic life values.

Individuals who are unreciprocating are likely to disagree about basic life values. Those who are reciprocating will tend to agree. Thus societies and groups whose members are extremely reciprocating in everyday interaction have high levels of social integration (agreement about life values). Those where members are extremely unreciprocating possess low levels of social integration.

At this juncture it will be well to return briefly to the theories of homicide outlined earlier and to consider in what ways they make use of reciprocity and social integration. Henry and Short refer implicitly to those ideas. Extreme one-sided restraints placed upon some persons by others mean a low level of integration of individuals into the social structure and a high degree of unreciprocity in everyday interaction. Some block others and in so doing not only fail to engage in reciprocity but go beyond neutrality to the opposite extreme of unreciprocity. Henry and Short suggest in effect that those who most feel the frustrating effects of these conditions become the homicidal offenders.

Straus and Straus give central emphasis to closeness and looseness of structuring of society. It can be interpreted that the more loosely is a society structured, the lower is social integration. Straus and Straus speak explicitly of reciprocity: The less are reciprocal rights and duties stressed and enforced, they say, the more loosely structured is the society. And the higher is the homicide rate.

Wood writes of relative deprivation in regard to strivings for upward mobility as a generator of homicide. Wide-scale blockage to upward mobility implies an "at loggerheads," unreciprocating way of life. It means broad differences in life values and low social integration.

Merton points to the anomic condition which results when there is a large disparity between cultural goals and institutionalized means for achieving them. There is unreciprocity between those who have access to means and those who are blocked. High levels of anomie indicate low levels of social integration. Cohen's focus is on the reaction-formation of lower-class boys to the goals-means disparity, to what might be termed socially structured unreciprocity. The values of the resulting delinquent subculture are flatly in opposition to the values of the prevailing overall culture. To the extent delinquent subcultures are strong, social integration is low.

Cloward and Ohlin's delinquent opportunity structures are characterized by value systems clearly at odds with legitimate opportunity structures. Low social integration is implied. To the degree that individuals are blocked from access to both delinquent and legitimate structures, structured unreciprocity is compounded.

Miller emphasizes that the high prestige classes make the legal rules and in so doing define lower-class aggression as criminal. Value differences between the classes are great and signify low integration. Further, the punishment of behavior indigenous to the lower classes by the higher classes implies much unreciprocity. Wolfgang and Ferracuti speak of widespread discrimination as one possible explanation of why subcultures of violence develop. Such discrimination is a form of structured unreciprocity. And the cleavage between violent subcultures and the dominant culture points to a lack of social integration.

Sykes and Matza focus on the tendency of lower-class boys to rationalize their violence and theft toward others. The boys point to the real or alleged unreciprocity of middle-class persons toward them. Status threats, discussed by Short and Strodbeck, can be seen as elements of unreciprocating interaction that may trigger violence. Porterfields's Index of Social Well-Being provides broad-scale measures of reciprocity and integration. The greater are the differences among the states in social well-being the higher will be the unreciprocity in the society as a whole. And the greater are the differences in well-being, the less will be the agreement over life values and the lower will social integration be.

Thus through the several theoretical approaches reviewed here there run quite distinctly the ideas of reciprocity, unreciprocity, and social integration. These ideas, especially reciprocity and unreciprocity, will constitute major elements of the analysis ahead. But they must be integrated with a number of other concepts, in particular those of role, situation, and social system.

9. *A Role Formulation of Homicide*

While the above theories do not for the most part deal explicitly with the matter, it is largely in role relationships that reciprocity and unreciprocity occur. And it is largely through roles that individuals share or do not share common life values and are to greater or lesser degree integrated with one another and with the larger society.

In a previous volume the concept of role and the related concept of status were discussed at length.[41] The views of Linton, Bennett and Tumin, Davis, Newcomb, Gross *et al.*, and others were reviewed. A status was seen as a position in social space denoted by a body of expectational norms for acting in that position. Role was defined as a group of performance patterns that are typical of all encumbents of a given status.[42] Statuses and roles exist always in pairs: for each status there is a role.

When statuses and roles are viewed in this way, the concern is not with expectations for a particular person or with simply his performances. Rather the concern is with expectations and performances as they transcend any given person. For example, the status and role of a police officer refer to the ways in which men acting as police officers are typically expected to behave and how typically they do behave. Attention will be given at a later point to the internalization of statuses and roles by particular individuals.

Statuses and roles, in the supraindividual sense indicated

above, are components of institutionalized social situations. A social situation is essentially an episode of interaction.[43] When interaction is patterned and recurs in similar form, the situation is said to be institutionalized. (A situation in which interaction is not patterned can be termed idiosyncratic.) Institutionalized situations are made up of two or more roles, and attendant statuses, that are oriented toward each other. Role performances constitute the patterned interaction of an institutionalized social situation.

Social situations can be seen as being in a greater or lesser state of tension. This means that the roles which constitute a situation are in tension with each other. And tension depends on reciprocity. The more do role performances in a given situation facilitate each other, the greater is reciprocity; and the lower is tension among the roles involved and in the situation. Conversely, the more do role performances block each other, the less is reciprocity; the greater is unreciprocity; and the higher is tension among roles and in the situation.

When tension in a situation is very low, participants smother in undue reciprocity. The stagnating effects of overintegration mean great frustration for the individuals involved. Yet all is well organized and ostensibly peaceful. There is no one to blame. Eventually the self comes to bear the responsibility and aggression is directed toward it.[44] The relationship between low tension and self-directed aggression is pursued at length in Part II and will be set side for the present.

Situations characterized by tension in the middle-range are difficult to find. Research projects, whether pure or applied, offer frequently apt illustrations of situations in moderate tension. Role performnces tend to be neither unduly reciprocating nor unreciprocating. Researchers challenge one another to a degree that stimulates constructive thought and self-criticism. They do not sit in stagnation as do participants in low tension situations. Neither are they preoccupied with resentment that crowds out innovation as is the case with those in the loggerheads interaction of high tension situations.

In situations of high tension, participants are under much strain to perform adequately. There is little integration of individuals with the group. Each participant tends to feel the others are blocking him from doing what he is expected to do. Each blames the others and each retaliates. The knot of unreciprocity tightens. Frustration runs very high. It is now that the situation verges on explosion. It is here that homicide is likely to occur. The greater the tension level of a situation, the greater the probability of homicide.

Now, institutionalized situations are bound together into social systems which themselves are in greater or lesser states of tension. Similarly, social systems combine to form whole societies. The details of how situations combine to form social systems and systems to form societies have been elaborated elsewhere.[45] Briefly, certain types of situations link together other situations into whole social systems. For example, situations involving the status and role of a prison guard and of an inmate leader may serve as connecting links between administrative situations and inmate situations and so may contribute to the formation of a prison social system. The degree of reciprocity or unreciprocity between role performances in the connecting situations determines the tension level of the system.

Regarding linkages between one social system and another, the same example can be followed: In a small state it may be customary for prison wardens to meet annually with the appropriations committee of the state legislature regarding prison budgetary allotments for the coming year. If so, such meetings will provide connecting links between the social systems of the prison and of the legislature. Again, reciprocity and unreciprocity between the role performances in the situations that link the systems will determine the tension level of the group of social systems, and in the ultimate of the society *per se*.[46] As with situations, the greater is unreciprocity in social systems or societies, the less are individuals likely to agree about life values and thus the lower will be social integration. And it is predicted that the higher the tension level of a social system or of a society as a whole, the greater will be the homicide rate.

In broad compass the theoretical formulation has been set that will guide the analysis. Attention turns now to pertinent data about social systems and situations in relation to homicide. In chapter three the formulation will be extended to embrace the internalization of roles by the individual.

CHAPTER II

Homicide and the Social System

1. *Homicide Rates in Literate Societies*

Rates for criminal homicide vary greatly among literate societies and among non-literate societies as well. Of the 61 literate societies in Table 1, *circa* 1960, annual rates range from the extraordinarily high figure of 34.0 per 100,000 of the population for Colombia to the equally extraordinary low of 0.2 for Ireland. The median rate is 1.8. In addition to Colombia, the Latin American countries of Mexico and Nicaragua have extremely high homicide rates of 31.1 and 22.8 respectively. South Africa too possesses an abnormally great rate of 21.2. In sharp contrast, the Netherlands have a very low rate of 0.3, Denmark and Norway of 0.5 each, England and Wales of 0.6, Iceland of 0.6 and Sweden of 0.7.

Generally speaking, countries with high homicide rates are characterized by political instability, by rapid change toward an industrialized state, and by groups within the society that oppose one another strongly. Colombia is a case in point. In this technologically developing country, major political parties have been involved in recent decades in a state of undeclared war. Feuding and killing have spread rapidly throughout many non-political groups as well. The proliferation of homicidal death has taken on the general name of the *violencia*. Annual rates of homicide in some sections of Colombia have reached 60.0 per 100,000 of the population. Of a total population of 14,000,000, over 200,000 persons have been murdered in the last several decades. Among young adults, homicide is the leading cause of death.[1]

At the other extreme are societies possessing political stability, a relatively slow rate of change and few groups in conflict with one another. The Northern European countries are illustrative. Iceland, for example, has a long history of exceedingly low

TABLE 1—*Homicide Rates In Literate Societies By Year of Report**

Rate per 100,000	Country	Year	Rate per 100,000	Country	Year
34.0	Colombia	1960	1.8	Singapore	1960
31.1	Mexico	1958	1.7	France	1960
22.8	Nicaragua	1959	1.6	Hungary	1960
21.2	South Africa	1959	1.5	Australia	1960
10.8	Burma	1959	1.5	Greece	1960
9.9	Aden Colony	1956	1.4	Canada	1960
9.8	Guatemala	1960	1.4	Italy	1959
6.1	Turkey	1959	1.2	Australasia	1960
5.9	Panama	1960	1.2	Jordan	1960
5.3	Puerto Rico	1959	1.1	New Zealand	1960
5.3	St. Vincent	1955	1.0	Hong Kong	1960
4.9	Chile	1957	0.9	Mauritius ex. dep.	1960
4.6	Uruguay	1955	0.9	Northern Ireland	1960
4.6	Trinidad/Tobago	1960	0.9	Portugal	1960
4.5	United States	1960	0.9	Switzerland	1959
4.4	Nigeria	1960	0.8	Spain	1959
4.3	Ceylon	1959	0.7	Belgium	1959
3.9	Dominican Republic	1955	0.7	Ryukyu Islands	1960
3.2	Costa Rica	1960	0.7	Scotland	1960
3.0	Channel Islands	1959	0.7	Sweden	1959
3.0	Reunion	1956	0.6	England/Wales	1960
2.9	Finland	1960	0.6	Iceland	1959
2.7	Bulgaria	1960	0.6	Luxembourg	1960
2.6	North Borneo	1960	0.6	Sarawak	1958
2.5	Barbados	1960	0.5	Cape Verde Islands	1959
2.3	United Arab Republic	1958	0.5	Denmark	1959
2.2	Perú	1959	0.5	Norway	1959
2.1	Poland	1959	0.4	British Guiana	1958
1.9	Japan	1960	0.3	Malta/Gozo	1960
1.8	Fed. Rep. of Germ.		0.3	Netherlands	1960
	West Berlin	1959	0.2	Ireland (Eire)	1960

*Marvin E. Wolfgang and Franco Ferracuti, *The Subculture of Violence* (London: Social Science Paperbacks), pp. 274-75. Original Source: Item BE5o (E964, E965, E980-E999) from *Demographic Yearbook*, Thirteenth Issue (New York: United Nations Publications, 1961), pp. 398-471.

homicide rates. It has also a history as a fiercely independent society whose members possess a rough-and-ready life style. A socialistic democracy, Iceland is characterized by a daily life that is neither unduly competitive nor cooperative. Role relations among Icelanders are marked by middle-range reciprocity. Tension in Icelandic social systems seems to be at neither extreme.

Individuals collide with each other, so to speak, but not with undue harshness.[2]

2. Non-Literate Societies and Homicide

Among non-literate societies, as among literate, much variation in homicide rates obtains. In a study by the author of 40 non-literate groups, rates ranged from an equivalent of about 10.0 per 100,000 population to zero.[3] The median rate for the non-literate societies was somewhat lower than for literate societies. Non-literate societies were also rated regarding the extent to which they emphasized reciprocity in role relations.[4] As Table 2 indicates, there was a clear tendency for reciprocity and homicide to be inversely related. Of the 19 societies that were above the median rating for homicide, 13 were below the median rating for reciprocity. (Some of those that were low on reciprocity stressed unreciprocity while others tended more toward neutrality in role relationships.) Of those same 19 societies, but six were above the median for reciprocity. And of the 21 societies below the median homicide rating, 14 were above the median rating for reciprocity while seven were below it.

Societies with much unreciprocity and high homicide rates were, as might be expected, extremely competitive and individualistically oriented. Two or more major groups in the society were likely to be strongly opposed to each other. Aggression in its various forms tended to be common and suspicion of others to run high. The Maori are illustrative.[5] Their traditional life showed cyclical periods of excessive competition, great unreci-

TABLE 2—*Numbers of Non-Literate Societies Above and Below Median Scores for Reciprocity in Role Relationships and for Homicide*

	Low Homicide (Below Median)	High Homicide (Above Median)	Total
High Reciprocity (Above Median)	14	6	20
Low Reciprocity* (Below Median)	7	13	20
Total	21	19	40

*Includes unreciprocity.

procity in role relations, a wide variety of aggressive behavior and suspicion verging on paranoia. Interestingly these periods of about a year's duration alternated with period of a similar length and quite different content. Maori life would take on a cooperative, reciprocating aspect in which individualistic tendencies were submerged in favor of group needs. The traditional Maori had extremely high suicide as well as homicide rates. These forms of violence seem to have been tied to the two phases of Maori life, homicide being a consequence of competitive unreciprocity and suicide of cooperative reciprocity.

Those non-literate societies with little or no homicide tend to be highly cooperative and uncompetitive. They seldom stress great differences in prestige. Their members are self-effacing and emphasize the importance of the society over the individual. The Indians of the Southwest United States are illustrative. Included are the Zuni, the Taos, the Hopi and to a lesser extent the Navaho and Papago. These societies, while certainly differing in particulars, reflect the characteristics just noted.[6] The Hopi, for example, place much stress on not winning; it is bad form to win.[7] In their much valued foot-races, a man should do all that he can to insure that he does not come in first. In most aspects of Hopi life, reciprocity in role relations runs very high.

3. *Geographical and Class Differences in the United States*

To turn now to the contemporary United States: With a rate of 4.5 in 1960, we ranked fifteenth from the top among the 61 countries listed in Table 1. By 1970 the United States rate had increased greatly to 7.8.[8] Variations by region of the country are substantial. Some regions have rates about four times as great as others. Table 3 indicates that in 1967 the three southern areas had the greatest rates, between 9.0 and 10.0 per 100,000 population. New England had the lowest rate, 2.4, of any section of the country. The state with the lowest criminal homicide rate in 1967 was Maine with a rate of 0.4; Alabama had the highest rate, 11.7.[9]

Disparities between success goals and access to the means for achieving them are especially great in the south. Poor whites and

blacks, blocked from achievement, live in close proximity to
middle- and upper-class whites.[10] In the south, the denial of
fundamental reciprocity to blacks by whites is as blatant as the
recurrent emphasis on superficial reciprocity. (By the latter is
meant the condescension of whites toward blacks; and the obse-
quious public posturing of some blacks toward whites.) In New
England, particularly upper New England, vestiges of the Puri-
tan ethic yield a considerable degree of reciprocity in role relations. While no doubt great changes will take place, presently
competition appears to be significantly less severe there than in
the country as a whole. And in New England racial problems
have not been as great as in other regions in part because there
have been relatively few blacks.

Traditionally homicide rates have been slightly higher in rural
than urban areas. Vold concluded that there seemed to be "a
tendency to higher rural rates in offenses against the person,
such as homicides, infanticides, and grave assaults.[11] At present
in the United States, however, rates are quite definitely highest
in the large cities, those with populations of 250,000 or more. In
1967, these cities had a criminal homicide rate of 11.9 per
100,000 population. Rural areas possessed a rate of 5.9 and
suburban areas the lowest rate, 3.3.[12] There would seem to be
considerable agreement among sociologists that reciprocity in
everyday life is on balance distinctly lower in the large cities
than in less densely populated places.[13] Familial, economic, educational and political social systems in high tension appear now
to be more characteristic of urbanized areas than of those that
are relatively rural.[14]

TABLE 3—*Criminal Homicide Rates by Geographical Region,
United States, 1967*°

New England	2.4	East South Central	9.2
Middle Atlantic	4.6	West South Central	9.2
North Central	4.9	Mountain	4.8
West North Central	3.7	Pacific	4.9
South Atlantic	9.6	Total	6.1

°Data taken from: Federal Bureau of Investigation, *Crime in the United
States, Uniform Crime Reports—1967* (U.S. Government Printing Office,
1968), pp. 62-67.

Considering the United States as a whole, it is probably fair to say that we are an extraordinarily competitive people. Many encounter great difficulty in making ends and means meet.[15] Significantly, there is in this and many other societies a clear inverse relationship between rates of criminal homicide and social class position of offenders (and of victims as well).[16] One study shows the fairly typical finding that in a five-class hierarchy, homicidal offenders are overrepresented in the lowest class by more than twice while they are greatly underrepresented in the higher classes.[17]

Unreciprocity in higher prestige circles takes more subtle forms than in the lower classes. Not infrequently the lower-class male is blocked from obtaining a job of any kind or from gaining further education.[18] In contrast the upper-middle-class male may, say, face the problem of whether he can gain admission to the college or university of his choice; or of whether he can get the particular job or the promotion he wants. The response of the upper-middle-class male to institutionalized unreciprocity is less likely than that of the lower-class male to take the form of physical attack. It is more likely to be symbolic of physical attack, to involve, say, an attempt to destroy the reputation, the credibility, of one who is perceived as blocking his economic and prestige strivings.

4. Racial Variations

Homicide rates vary widely by race, age and sex. Regarding race: There is in the United States considerable discrimination against blacks in arrests for homicide. Whites are less often convicted. And blacks are more often erroneously convicted.[19] On the other hand, there is a tendency in the northern ghettos and in the southern towns for officials to look the other way when blacks kill blacks.[20] Overall, race relations variables cannot account for much of the great differences in homicide rates for whites and blacks.

Rates of homicide in the black ghettos of the United States are frequently 50 times or more those in the white upper-middle-class suburbs.[21] Across the country as a whole, black arrest rates for homicide as reported by the Federal Bureau of Investigation are 12 times those for whites.[22] Stearns's data for Massachusetts showed that 10 per cent of homicidal offenders were black while but one per cent of the state's population was black.[23] Meyers analyzed murderous offenders in St. Louis and found rates of 33.0 for blacks and 2.5 for whites.[24] In Wolfgang's Philadelphia study, blacks had a criminal homicide rate of 24.6 compared to that of 1.8 for whites.[25]

Blacks are, in relation to whites, especially blocked from achieving prestigious occupations in the professional, technical and managerial fields. In 1967, non-whites (the vast majority of whom are black) were three times as likely as whites to be in non-farm laboring jobs and one third as likely as whites to hold professional, technical or managerial positions.[26] Six percent of white workers were employed as non-farm laborers compared to 20 per cent of non-whites. In professional, technical and managerial occupations, there were 27 per cent of white workers as contrasted with nine per cent of non-whites.

While individuals do not necessarily aspire to gain a high school or college education in itself, that education is a prerequisite for most prestigious occupational and social class roles. As of 1960 in the United States non-whites had completed 8.2 years of school and whites 10.8 years.[27] Twenty-two per cent of non-whites and twice as great a proportion of whites, 43.0 per cent, had finished high school. Proportional to numbers, well over twice as many whites as non-whites had completed college, the respective percentages being 8.1 and 3.5.[28]

In 1966, the median family income for blacks was but 58 per cent of that for whites.[29] Growth in black family income is not keeping pace with growth for whites. In constant 1965 dollars, the median non-white family income in 1947 was $2174 less than that for white familities. By 1966, the gap had increased to $3036.[30] Twenty per cent of black persons, those with the lowest incomes, are making no significant economic gains whatsoever.[31] Further, non-whites seeking employment are much less able to find jobs than are whites. In 1950, the unemployment rate for non-whites was 7.9 per cent; for whites the figure was 4.5 per cent. In 1960 the figures had risen to 10.2 and 5.0 per cent respectively.[32]

The percentage of non-whites living in poverty (as defined by the Social Security Administration) in central cities of metropolitan areas was 41.7 in 1964. For whites, the figure was 23.8.[33] Fifty-four per cent of all children in poverty families in those central cities were non-white.[34] Closely attached to the condition of poverty is the infant mortality rate. In 1965 and proportionate to their numbers in the population, over half again as many non-white as white babies died before one month of age. The white rate was 16.1 per 1000 live births while for non-whites it was 25.4. The mortality rate for infants one month to one year of age was two-and-a-half times as great for non-whites as for whites. The respective rates (per 1000 live births) were 14.9 and 5.4.[35]

It has come into the national consciousness but recently that race relations in the United States have consisted largely of a one-way reciprocity that has greatly favored whites at the expense of blacks. This has been true in all regions of the country. In the large urbanized places, unreciprocity and tension are high not only in situations where blacks and whites come together. They are high also in those ghetto situations that involve only blacks. The depth of poverty, the futility of attempted achievement and the absence of hope in the black ghetto are well known and require no further documentation. It is less well recognized that blacks in the ghettos kill one another much more frequently than official statistics indicate.[36] As noted, there is a tendency for officials to ignore such deaths. Thus homicidal violence becomes accepted officially as well as informally.

It is even less well understood that life in the ghetto is in many respects a sequence of widely fluctuating degrees of situational tension. Saturday is the time of what pleasantry there is with money in the pockets of some. Then with late Saturday night and the early hours of Sunday morning comes the high point of unreciprocity and tension. Brawls, assaults that escalate into death are common compared to most segments of society. The pains of countless slights at the hands of whites and of attempts, blocked by whites, to grasp slivers of success translate themselves into violence. Reciprocity is denied those who are there—other blacks—by blacks. Blacks become the targets for the rage that is felt toward whites. The great upsurge of high tension in the ghetto at week's end is more frustrating than would be a generally high state of tension characterized by lesser shifts in the level of that tension.

The roller coaster that is the social system of the ghetto runs downward through Sunday night. On Monday morning all is as still as the aftermath of a nuclear explosion. Some sleep off the weekend; some stare from windows. Some on their way to work make way wordlessly in the filth-laden tenement halls for others bound also for work. Interaction is low and what there is of it is characterized by high reciprocity. This signals the beginning of the boredom, the nothingness, the meaninglessness of the week. It is a time for self-directed violence and, at the extreme, for suicide. While black suicide rates have in general been found to be low throughout the society, recent evidence points to high rates in the ghettos, especially for young adult males.[37] The dynamics of this phenomenon are discussed in later chapters.

5. *Variations by Sex and Age*

Almost universally homicidal offenders tend to a significant degree to be males. In the United States, male rates have been reported from three to nine times as high as female rates. Meyers found that 74 per cent of homicidal offenders were male.[38] Harlan found 76 per cent to be male.[39] Cassidy's findings show the percentage to be 90 and Dublin and Bunzel put the figure at 93.[40] In his Philadelphia study, Wolfgang states that 82 per cent of offenders were male.[41] The Federal Bureau of Investigation reports that in 1967 the ratio of arrests for murder was more than five males for every one female.[42] Templewood writes that 68 per cent of offenders in England and Wales over a 49-year period were male.[43] Elwin found a high proportion of male offenders among the Maria.[44] In seven non-literate African societies, Bohannan reports findings of a very high (over nine-tenths) proportion of male offenders.[45] And in a study of 54 non-literate societies around the world, male offenders clearly predominated in most of the societies; in some societies, numbers of male and female offenders were about equal; in no case did the female offenders clearly predominate.[46]

Durkheim spoke of women as "being less deeply involved in the struggle for life."[47] Mabel Elliott holds that "the average woman experiences less conflict between her ethical values (and mode of life) and the achievement of her goals than does the average man."[48] Certainly it does seem reasonable to contend that in the United States and often elsewhere as well, males are engaged in competitive and at times highly unreciprocating interaction to a considerably greater extent than females.[49]

Age of offender is also an extremely critical variable in homicide. Henry and Short give data for the United States for 1950 as shown in Table 4. And Wolfgang reports rates by age for his Philadelphia study (Table 5). Data from the Uniform Crime Reports and from works by Durkheim,[50] Hoffman,[51] and Brearly,[52] provide much the same pattern. That pattern is one of low homicide rates in childhood, a heavy concentration in the early adult years and a gradual decline over the succeeding decades of life. Rates among those in their twenties are about five times as high as among those fifty years of age or more. Societies around the world tend to conform to this pattern. The previously mentioned study of non-literate societies indicates a strong predominance of homicidal offenders among young adult age groups, somewhat less in middle age and least in old age and childhood.[53]

TABLE 4—*Homicides per 100,000 Population in the United States, by Age—1950**

Age Group	Homicide Rate
All ages	4.20
15-19	4.84
20-24	10.27
25-29	9.84
30-34	8.14
35-39	7.16
40-44	5.84
45-49	4.78
50 and over	1.91

*Adapted from Andrew F. Henry and James F. Short, Jr., *Suicide and Homicide* (New York: The Free Press, 1964), p. 89.

TABLE 5—*Homicides per 100,000 Population in Philadelphia, Annual Averages by Age for 1948-1952*[*]

Age	Rate	Age	Rate
Under 15	0.3	45-49	7.8
15-19	9.4	50-54	3.0
20-24	12.6	55-59	3.2
25-29	11.9	60-64	2.0
30-34	11.1	65 and over	1.3
35-39	9.7	All ages	6.0
40-44	7.6		

[*]Marvin E. Wolfgang, *Patterns in Criminal Homicide* (Philadelphia: University of Pennsylvania Press, 1958), p. 66.

It is in early adulthood that individuals are most likely to come up against insurmountable social blockages to their aspirations for the successful playing out of their roles. For the adolescent, at least for the individual in the earlier years of adolescence, there is the hope that somehow aspirations will later be met. For some they will. For others, the first years of adulthood become a time when it is clearly indicated that the gates to role achievement have slammed shut. The frustration of this institutionalized unreciprocity, this socially structured relative deprivation, is very great. To the extent that the deprived individuals perceive that others are responsible for that frustration, aggression will be outward and, in extreme cases, homicidal. To the degree that the self is held responsible, aggression will be inward and suicidal.

6. Age, Sex, and Race in Relation to One Another

Wolfgang's Philadelphia findings are representative of national patterns. As Table 6 shows, in all age categories black male rates exceed rates for black females, for white males and for white females. Rates for black males are over 60.0 per 100,000 population for each age category between 15 and 40 years. The highest rate, 92.5, is for those black males aged 20 to 24. This is more than 300 times greater than the lowest reported rate. 0.3, which is for white females in the 40-44 years age range. At all age levels except 15 to 19 years, black female rates exceed white male rates. In the 25 to 29 years age category, the black female

TABLE 6—*Criminal Homicide Rate by Age, Race and Sex of Offender, Philadelphia, 1948-1952**

| | | Black | | | White | |
Age	Total	Male	Female	Total	Male	Female
Under 15	.4	.4	.4	.2	.3	—
15-19	38.0	79.2	2.9	2.5	4.6	.4
20-24	46.6	92.5	12.4	4.6	8.2	1.2
25-29	47.4	77.8	22.3	2.5	4.6	.6
30-34	44.3	75.1	19.3	2.8	5.2	.6
35-39	35.4	65.5	9.8	3.3	6.0	.9
40-44	30.0	47.1	14.6	2.4	4.7	.3
45-49	30.8	44.0	18.2	2.5	4.4	.7
50-54	15.9	29.4	1.9	.5	1.1	—
55-59	19.7	30.6	8.5	.8	1.7	—
60-64	5.9	7.9	4.0	1.5	2.6	.5
65 and over	6.0	10.5	2.2	.8	1.8	—
All ages	24.6	41.7	9.3	1.8	3.4	.4

*From Marvin E. Wolfgang, *Patterns in Criminal Homicide* (Philadelphia: University of Pennsylvania Press, 1958), p. 66.

rate of 22.3 is five times the white male rate of 4.6. And that rate of 22.3 for black females is extremely high in comparison to rates for homicide in general, whether in this or other societies.

It was mentioned earlier that if blockage to achievement of success goals occurs, it is likely to be greatest in early adulthood. And for black males this will tend to be especially so. Young black males may have vague dreams of glory in adolescence but a few years later many will be confronted with the inevitability of socio-economic failure. As for black females in young adulthood, they are likely to have several children whom they attempt to support with an unskilled job. The fathers of the children are often either permanently absent or home only sporadically. The women are caught squarely in the social structural bind of having to fend for themselves and their children in a hostile economy, hostile in that the only jobs available are very often low-paying and physically and emotionally taxing. It is an open question whether these black females are more vulnerable than white males to societally built-in denial of reciprocity, particularly as it concerns economic and prestige matters. Certainly of the four age-sex groups the white female appears to be the least vulnerable. Whatever else her life difficulties, and they are considerable,[54] she is highly unlikely to be on the receiving end of the extremes of blocked, loggerheads interaction.

It is, then, the oppressed who are the homicidal. The poor, the uneducated, those without legitimate opportunities, respond to their institutionalized oppression with outward explosions of aggression. Gradually there is created a subculture and a social system of violence.[55] In the black ghettos and in other poverty areas, it is close at hand. And when the oppressed experience sufficiently severe stress, they turn to the patterns of that subculture.

7. *Victim and Offender*

The nature of the immediate situations and circumstances surrounding homicidal violence is of much importance in any rounded understanding of the phenomenon. Regarding the victim-offender relationship: As a rule the two individuals are friends or acquaintances and often they are biologically related or are marital partners.[56]

A cross-cultural study indicates that in the vast majority of non-literate societies analyzed, 41 out of 44, homicidal victims and offenders are rarely if ever strangers.[57] Among 550 Philadelphia homicide cases, Wolfgang found that victim and offender were close friends in 28.2 per cent of the killings; in 24.7 per cent they were relatives; in 13.5 percent they were acquaintances; in another 9.8 per cent they were paramours; and in but 12.2 were they strangers. (The remaining percentages included homosexual partners, police officer-felon relationship, and so on.)[58] For the United States as a whole, 29 per cent of all murders in 1966 occurred between offender and victim who were members of the same family.[59] Slightly over half of those cases involved one spouse killing the other; in about one seventh of the cases, parents killed their children.

When victims and offenders have never met, the offender is nonetheless likely to be familiar with the victim's characteristics or with the characteristics of individuals like the victim. For example, two young men despise middle-class values. They choose a family well known in the locality for its personification of those values. The men are not personally acquainted with the family but they know much about them. They go to the family's home and kill all members.[60] Again a college student who feels out of place and snubbed by his peers climbs to the top of a campus tower.[61] He shoots to death a number of students crossing the yard below. While they have been individually unknown to him, the victims represent, personify, those whom he sees as his frustrators.

Regarding assassinations, while in most cases the offender has never talked with his victim, the victim is likely to symbolize to him some group of persons or some general condition that he has conceived to be a severe threat. Thus Sirhan Sirhan, a Jordanian with strong negative feelings toward Israel, saw Robert Kennedy, who spoke favorably of Israel, as his enemy.[62] Martin Luther King was the leader of a movement hated by his assassin, James Earl Ray. While the relationship of Lee Harvey Oswald to John Kennedy is less clear, there is some evidence to indicate that the young President represented everything successful and debonair that Oswald found himself not to be.[63]

As is well established in research reports, race of victim and offender is likely to be the same. Wolfgang states: "In 94 per cent of the 550 identified relationships, the victim and offender were members of the same race: 72 per cent of the total were Negro and 22 per cent white. Of these 516 homicides involving members of the same race, 77 per cent were Negro and 23 per cent white. Hence, in only 34, or 6 per cent, of the homicides did an offender cross the race line...."[64] Harlan found that of 500 homicides in Birmingham, Alabama, but three per cent were interracial.[65] And Meyers, reporting on some 200 cases, also puts the figure at three per cent.[66] Garfinkel's study of 821 homicidal cases gives a figure of nine per cent.[67]

Blacks kill blacks even though whites are perceived by them as major sources of unreciprocity and hence of frustration. The upward spiral of unreciprocity and high tension and the consequent explosion take place in confrontational situations, often repeated situations, that tend to be a usual part of everyday life. And that everyday life is largely intraracial. Black comes to stand for white because of situational necessity. Especially will this be so when both potential victims and offenders feel strongly the oppression of whites. Each aggresses against the other because the other is there. This is likely to mean a greater or lesser degree of victim-precipitation wherein victim aggresses against offender as well as offender against victim.[68]

There may come the time when these patterns weaken and whites become the victims of black aggression in much greater numbers. Increasing intermingling of the two races may facilitate this shift. For then white will be the immediate target for past unreciprocity toward black. This does not mean that greater interaction between the races should be discouraged. It is simply an informally stated hypothesis. In any event, the racial problems of this society provide a primary example of the general condition of denied reciprocity as a major generating force of homicide.

8. Victim-Precipitation

In the United States and elsewhere as well, homicide tends to occur in the context of a quarrel or where insult or jealousy is clearly present.[69] Two major patterns emerge here. First there is a sudden argument between two persons who, while they know each other, do not interact daily. One resorts to extreme violence. For example two men run across each other in a bar. One accuses the other of having molested his wife some time ago. They fight; one pulls a knife and kills the other. This is less usual than the second form where there is a daily mounting buildup of argument and insult over weeks, months, or years.[70] Finally, one participant breaks that process by bringing about the death of the other.

Often it is difficult to determine to what extent the victim "conspires" with the offender, helping to bring about his own demise.[71] Tarde wrote at some length of the phenomenon of victim-precipitation.[72] More recently von Hentig,[73] Wolfgang,[74] and Shafer[75] among others have given the matter sustained attention. Wolfgang has made the most extensive empirical investigation.[76] Of 588 homicidal cases in his analysis, 150 or 26 per cent were victim-precipitated. Wolfgang confined his definition of victim-precipitation to those interchanges resulting in death where the victim was the first to use physical force. If he had been able to include serious psychological provocation, the percentage of victim-precipitated cases would undoubtedly have been considerably higher.

In any event, Wolfgang found offenders tended to be female and victims to be male. Both victims and offenders were more likely to be black than white. Offenders and victims were often related. Moreover, Wolfgang found that in a disproportionately large number of victim-precipitated slayings, offenders were wives and victims were their husbands. Typically the male lashed out assaultively at the female and she retaliated in the extreme.[77] The spiral of conflict was broken by a final clash, physically initiated by the victim, that had within it elements of an inverted reciprocity: victim and offender were cooperating in the former's death.

9. *Weapons, Places, and Times*

Apart from whether victim-precipitation is involved, especially lethal weapons such as firearms, knives, and clubs are typically used to carry out the homicidal act.[78] Generally these weapons are employed in a frenzied attack upon the victim. And not infrequently the attack is more than sufficient to kill.[79] However, less physically aggressive means, poisoning for example, are not uncommon.[80] Whatever the weapon, the carefully planned, highly rational killing is a rarity in the United States and in most other societies.[81]

To what extent the unavailability of firearms and other weapons might decrease homicide rates is largely unknown.[82] Ready access to lethal weapons may in some instances serve to convert what would have been assaults into criminal homicides.[83] However, many potential weapons are likely to be near at hand unless precautions are taken that unduly restrict ordinary activities of everyday life. For example, female offenders frequently make violent use of carving and other knives from the kitchen. To place bans on the possession of those would hardly be practicable.

Homicide seldom occurs in highly public places. The usual site is a home or other non-public place.[84] The bedroom and the kitchen are common scenes of attack.[85] Apart from dwelling places, the car is a fairly frequent setting.[86] To the extent that public places—streets, parks, and the like—may be the scenes of homicide, good lighting at night reduces the probability of death there.[87] What is unknown is the extent to which homicide within dwellings and cars may increase when lighting facilities in public are improved.

Homicide quite definitely predominates at night, in the early morning and on the weekend. This is true both in and out of the ghetto. Fridays, Saturdays, and Sundays from 8:00 p.m. to 2:00 a.m. are the times of highest rates.[88] As discussed earlier, these tend to be times of much unreciprocity. Also, and relatedly, they are times when individuals are most likely to have been consuming alcohol. About half of criminal homicide offenders in the United States have been drinking just prior to the killing.[89] So have about half of their victims.[90] Studies in other large societies show similar results.[91] While no brief is held here for alcohol as a fundamental "cause" of homicide, it can to some degree be a precipitating factor. As Wolfgang and Ferracuti say: "Not all intoxicated subjects become violent. Alcohol appears to be merely a releaser of violent traits and forms of behavior which are ordinarily kept under cortical control.[92]

In conclusion this can be said: Criminal homicide is on balance an intensely personal crime directed against those who are perceived as foremost threats by offenders or against those who symbolize such persons. Victims tend to be perceived as sources of blockage in the offenders' attempts to carry out adequately their social roles. There are clear indications that homicide occurs in those societies and social systems where because of unreciprocity tension is greatest and rises most abruptly. Within given social systems, homicide will predominate in those situations characterized by the most extreme high levels, and increases in levels, of tension.

10. *The Case of Louella Feary*

There follows the case of an aging woman, Louella Feary. The killing of her husband is an apt example of victim-precipitated homicide. Interviewed by the author in prison, she tells her story:

"What kind of a man was Feary? He was a son-of-a-bitch, that's what he was. A regular son-of-a-bitch. I don't usually use such words but with him I can't help myself. Oh, he was so nice on the outside, you know. He was one of those people, butter wouldn't melt in his mouth, and underneath he was as dirty and rotten as they come. He owned a farm up there, two hundred and forty acres, and you'd have thought he was something the way he put on. He was going to take me away from all of the trouble I'd seen. He took me in, I will say that for him. He took me in. Anyway we were married in the summer of 1940 and I moved up to the farm to live with him. Well, it was a mess, I tell you. Nice house on the outside but nothing inside. Furniture all broken down. I moved in my furniture, some of it pretty good. Feary had been short of money all along, and he told me one night soon after I'd moved in that he was planning on burning the barn.

"See, he was one of these people that would work pretty hard for a week or so and then he'd go off on a drunk for a couple of weeks. That's the way he did all the time. Work hard when he worked, drunk as a pig when he drank.

"The first while, him and me got along pretty good even with his drinking. But then pretty soon he got to cussing me out. No matter what I did he'd cuss me out. Why he's called me a whore more times than there's whores in the whole state. And that's plenty, believe me. Called me stupid, called me a liar, a cheat, thief, anything you can think of and a lot more. He called me them things time after time till I got sick and sick of hearing it. And like I told you, I'm sensitive and it made me feel awful.

"Feary and one friend or another was always taking off in the truck, the farm truck. Going somewhere or another to have a good time, get liquored up. I lived with that man for eight years and I tell you, life was nothing but one hell all of the time. He'd come home drunk and he'd cuss me out, and he'd hit me. One time he almost choked me to death. He was six foot-two, weighed a hundred and ninety pounds and there wasn't a thing I could do.

"Then as the time went on he got so he was mean even when he wasn't drinking. He'd sit there in the kitchen and cuss me up one side and down the other. Tell me what a whore I was, what a thief I was, a liar and all the rest of it. Many's the time I thought to myself, I could kill him. And most all this time I kept on working for one family or another. Doing housework and getting good money for it, too. Most of what we lived on came from what I made.

"Then in 1948 it was, I'd had enough. I couldn't take it from him any more and I left. Went to live in Toland. I was there five months when Feary came around just as sweet as you please. Oh, he was going to be so different. Butter wouldn't melt in his mouth. He wasn't going to touch a drop of liquor. Ever. He was going to treat me nice. Never call me names. Never cuss me out, swear at me again. Well, like a fool I believed it. I went back to live with him.

"Wasn't ten days after I'd been back he was cussing me out just like he had before. Calling me every filthy name in the book. Drinking again, threatening to beat me. I remember one time we got in an argument about something and Feary came up to me and stood there in front of me aad he just kept taking his right fist and smashing it into his left fist and saying, 'I ought to kill you.'

"Then, a couple of months later my son came to live with us. His wife had died and he didn't want to be alone. A week after that Feary decided he was going to take the cows down and sell them at this auction. So he got my son to help him get the cows loaded in the truck. Feary's way of getting cows in a truck was to drive the truck up to a stone-wall, back it up to the stone-wall, drop the tail-gate and let the cows climb in as best they could. Well this time he backed it up to a manure pile and he tried to get the cows in. There was three of them. They wouldn't go. They weren't having any part of it. But finally he got two of them in. The third one—the black one—wouldn't go and Feary was getting madder and madder. He was cussing me out to beat the band, cussing my son out and screaming at the cow.

"Finally Feary got a rope and he put it around the cow's mouth so the cow could hardly breathe. He told my son to take one end of the rope and get up in the truck and my son got up there. Then Feary, he got the pitchfork, and he got behind the cow and he started jabbing at her with the pitchfork. That cow could hardly breathe. You could hear it wheezing. But the cow wasn't having any part of going up in that truck. Well, Feary kept at it with the pitchfork but that cow wouldn't move up in the truck. Jabbing, jabbing, jabbing. Harder and harder. And Feary bellowing all the time. After five or ten minutes of that the cow fell down. You could hear it still wheezing. Then all of a sudden it shuddered and it lay still.

"My son called out, 'You killed her!'

" 'Serves the goddamned thing right,' says Feary.

"And he had killed it too. He killed it with that pitchfork. When he'd seen that he killed it he raised the pitchfork up over his head with both hands and brought it down on the head of that cow. He brought it down so hard he broke the handle of the pitchfork. The police chief, he got that broken pitchfork later, but he wouldn't bring it into court because he was one of Feary's boozing friends.

"Well, Feary got in the truck and he was bound and determined to take the other two cows down to the auction. 'Lou, get in the truck,' he yelled at me, not calling me Louella like he should.

"I just stood there. 'Lou, get in the goddamned truck,' he yelled again. I still didn't move and he jumped out of the truck. He came up to me, grabbed me by the shoulders and said, 'Now get in the goddamned truck or you'll be laying there just like that cow.'

"I got in, feeling numb all over from what he'd done to that cow. We went down the road, a dirt road it was, sixty miles an hour. Those two cows were laying down in the back but they were bouncing off the floor of the truck by as much as a foot. That's how fast he went down that dirt road. Wild man, that's what he was.

"When we got home I was sick, sick from seeing that cow killed like it was. I had to go to bed. I was shaking all over. Well, Feary went out drinking that night. And when he got home he came in the room and said, 'You're getting out. I'm having no more to do with you. I've got other women I can get to live here. I don't need you.'

"I told him I'd had the doctor earlier that evening, which I had. And he says, 'That don't make no difference. You're getting out.'

"For the next couple of days I couldn't eat a thing. I was so nervous I couldn't touch food. Then on the third day after that my son had to go to Toland and I got up and made breakfast for him. He could hardly eat himself from the thought of that cow and I couldn't eat anything. Feary was out drinking somewhere. He'd been out all night. I got my son off to Toland. That afternoon Feary came in, drunk as a skunk. He started cussing me out again. Knocking me around. I'd had just about enough. So later that afternoon I drove into town and on the way back I stopped and got me a nice little pistol in the gun store. I brought it home and put it in the dresser in my room.

"I wasn't planning on killing him, you see. I got it just to defend myself against him.

"Well, the next evening Feary came in to his dinner and I didn't have dinner ready. I didn't know he was coming in at that time. He yelled, 'Where the hell is dinner?' And so I told him how I'd been sick and he said, 'I told you to get out.' Well, he started abusing me once again. He started calling me every name in the book. Oh, what a whore I was and all of that stuff.

"I just slipped into my room and I took that pistol out of the dresser drawer and I loaded it. I slipped it into the pocket of my skirt underneath my apron. So he couldn't see it. I went back out into the kitchen. He was sitting in that big chair where he always sat and he started to cuss me out again.

"I went over to him, trying to put my arm around him, trying to make up. I was giving it one more try. Well, as I tried to put my arm around him he raised up and swung at me and hit me along side the head with his fist.

"I reeled back and then I pulled the gun. I hadn't had the safety catch on and I fired at him point blank. He was standing up as the bullet hit him and he staggered and went around the room in a big circle, tottering, and came right back to where he'd been before. 'You've done it now, Lou,' he said. 'You've really done it.' And with that he fell down straight out on the floor. Flat on his face. I took the gun and fired at him once more. Don't know what made me do it the second time. I guess I was just so mad at him for all the trouble he'd caused me.

"Then after I'd shot him for the second time I sat down in kind of a daze. I sat there not knowing what was going on. The fire went out and it grew awful cold. It must have been four or five hours later I came to, and almost freezing to death. The dog was there in the kitchen whimpering and whining away. I opened the door and he went out and we never saw him again. He wouldn't go back to the kitchen.

"I went into my room and laid down. And I was thinking to myself: Well, Feary, you got yours and got it good and you deserved it for all you've done to me. The next morning my son came home and he saw what I'd done.

"How do I feel about it, now? Killing him? He deserved it. Can you say different? That man was the meanest man on this earth. He made my life one hell from the day I met him."

CHAPTER III

Homicide and the Individual

1. *The Inner Roles of the Individual*

In this chapter, the theoretical formulation developed earlier is first extended to embrace the individual actor, particularly in regard to his learning and internalizing of statuses and of roles. Various data on the life histories of homicidal offenders are then surveyed in the light of that extended formulation. Special attention is given to early life frustration and the absence of role models as they affect the learning of roles. The places of identity and delusion in the development of homicidal individuals are traced. Finally, analysis is made of the conjunctions of conditions in the individual and the society that are especially likely to give rise to homicide.

Turning now to statuses and roles from the standpoint of a given person: Take away an individual's statuses and roles and what is left? Very little. Brim holds that the human personality is simply the sum total of the individual's internalized roles.[1] Even if one is unwilling to accept that position, it remains that roles, statuses and roles, are crucial to a person's social being and if they are taken away, the personality is drastically ravaged.

Everyone possesses inner status and role pairs which are the internalized counterparts of situational statuses and roles. An inner status is composed of the individual's typical expectations regarding his own performance in the particular status. An inner role is made up of the individual's typical perceptions of his performance in playing the given role. Self-expectations and self-perceived performances are, then, the content of inner status and role pairs.[2]

The inner status and role system of an individual is composed of all his inner status and role pairs during a given period in his life. That system is also in tension to a greater or lesser degree

50

although in a way quite different from a social situation. As discussed in the preceding chapter, tension in a situation is dependent upon the extent to which performances between the roles involved are reciprocating or unreciprocating. Reciprocity and unreciprocity are not directly at issue in the inner system. Tension in the inner system is a consequence of the degree to which the individual perceives that performances in his various inner roles interfere and conflict with one another.[3] The greater the perceived interference among those performances, the higher will be tension in the inner system.

Everyone is familiar with the necessity of a requisite degree of tension if an arch is to stand. Too much tension and the arch will come apart under the strain. Too little and it will collapse because of lack of strain. So it is with the inner system. As tension in that system grows very high, the individual is likely to experience great frustration because of the excessive strain of one role performance pulling against another. Alternately, as inner tension becomes very low, frustration tends to result because of the lack of tension: Each role performance is perceived as so easily carried out, so free of friction that an inner state of emptiness obtains. There is slackness, a lack of inner tone. That is, when tension in the inner system is exceedingly low, then the individual will experience much frustration, much anxiety. If, however, inner tension is in the middle range, then performance of any one of the individual's various roles will tend to be in rewarding contention with the performance of any other, not an impossible contention but rather one capable of being met.

The individual learns and internalizes statuses and roles in part by imitating others who serve as role models.[4] Other things equal, the more do role models act in accordance with typical performance patterns of the situational role in question, the more will the individual tend to act in that way. That is, the more will his performance be conforming. Further, the more will he tend to develop self-expectations that are similar to those that others hold; and the more will he perceive his own performances as conforming.[5]

"Other things" that may not be equal refer in the main to the rewards and frustrations set forth by other persons toward the given individual.[6] He will learn to perform in ways that have been rewarded. He will tend to perceive his performances much as others have indicated through reward and frustration sanctions that they have perceived those performances. And he will develop self-expectations that mirror his perceptions of his earlier performances in the role; he expects that he will do that which he believes he has done.

Again, other things equal, if unreciprocity between a given situational role and other situational roles has been high, then by definition it will be difficult for the individual to perform that role.[7] Thus the individual will be likely to perceive the role performance as one fraught with difficulties. And the more he views his performances in his different roles as difficult, the more conflict is he likely to perceive among those performances. Difficulty in one draws time and energy away from the adequate performance of others.

All of this means that while there will be individual differences, as a rule the more unreciprocity in regard to the situational roles that the individual internalizes and performs, the more conflict will he perceive among the roles that constitute his inner system. Put differently, the greater the tension in the situations in which the individual takes part, the greater tension will be in his inner role system.

Regarding social integration, it was said earlier that the higher the tension in a situation, social system, or society the more likely that participants will disagree about basic life values and the lower will be integration. Generally speaking, then, the higher the tension in the inner system of an individual, the less will he be integrated with his social environment.

Returning to matters of criminal homicide, one would predict that the higher the tension in the inner system of the individual, the greater the probability that he will commit homicide. Considering the inner system of the individual in conjunction with conditions in the surrounding social environment, this is predicted: Given high tension levels in a situation, social system or society, homicide is most likely to be committed by those individual participants whose inner systems are in greatest tension.

The concern in the pages ahead is with data that bear directly or indirectly on these hypotheses.

2. *Frustration in the Early Lives of Homicidal Offenders*

There are two especially striking facts about the early life histories of those who later commit homicide. Their childhoods are characterized by extreme physical and psychological frustrations. And the parental figure of the same sex as the offender tends to be absent from the home or markedly passive; while the parent of the opposite sex is likely to be present and dominant.[9]

In a study of homicide in New England, the early life experiences of 51 male offenders were compared with those of a control group composed of the nearest-age brothers of each of the offenders.[10] Severe birth traumas were two-and-a-half times more prevalent among offenders than control subjects. The offenders suffered in early life over four times as many serious surgical operations as their brothers, three-and-a-half times as much severe illness, and four times as many serious accidents. Regarding the last, falling on the head was particularly common. Parents beat the offenders somewhat more frequently than they beat the brothers.

The New England research indicated that toilet training was more abrupt and severe in cases of offenders than brothers. Sexual training was highly repressive for both groups of subjects. The homicidal group manifested significantly more phobias, compulsions, bed-wetting, sleepwalking, and nightmares than did the control subjects.[11]

Interaction between the New England offenders as children and their mothers was characterized by continual exchanges of implicit or explicit aggression. Difficulties and antagonisms between them were greater in number and intensity than they were between mothers and control brothers. As noted, the offenders' births were often traumatic; they were traumatic for the mother as well as the infant. In the early months of the offenders' lives, mothers and children were both often ill. The infants did not eat properly. The mothers were not strong enough to care for the new-born and yet there was no one else to do so. The children's illnesses irritated the mothers and the mothers' illnesses resulted in irritation for the children.[12]

A spiraling interplay of unreciprocity was set in motion between mother and child. The mother tended to blame the child. She would withdraw emotionally as a means of punishment. Crying, she would lock herself in her room and remain there for hours or in some cases days. The child would retaliate at a later point with unruly behavior. The mother would tend to ignore the child when danger threatened. Many of the aforementioned accidents that befell the children were in part the result of "negligence" by the mother. Mothers put the children's carriages at the tops of stairs where they would topple down. Mothers left the children unattended with knives and matches.[13]

Those who committed homicide in the New England study employed aggression releases in childhood about as often as the control brothers. However, the offenders showed a strong tendency to use releases classified as socially unacceptable while the brothers used predominantly those classified as acceptable. As examples, offenders stole, swore, lied to their mothers, intentionally hurt animals, and engaged in severe temper tantrums with distinctly greater frequency than did their brothers. Offenders tended to have histories of occasional but marked outbursts of physical aggression and the brothers did not. Offenders, often quiet children a great proportion of the time, might suddenly mutilate and kill an animal such as a cat or dog. They might grab a smaller child and repeatedly bang his head against the sidewalk. The social unacceptability of the potential offender's aggression releases, whether of minor or major proportion, tended to increase the frustration that they experienced. Others, in particular the mothers, were likely to find the offender's behavior threatening and to respond aggressively.[14]

The mothers of the New England offenders were in general exceedingly conscious about prestige matters. The vast majority were in the lower socio-economic classes. Their upward mobility strivings were very strong and almost invariably completely frustrated. The same was true of the offenders. Both offenders and mothers were acutely conscious of their failures in this regard. Both tended to blame others for that failure, to see others as having blocked their aspirations. The control brothers, on the other hand, were rather successful at moving up in the social class hierarchy.[15]

A number of studies tend to corroborate these findings as to the undue prevalence of physical and psychological frustrations in the life histories of homicidal offenders.[16] Endara reports that the mother-son relationship in homicidal cases has been severely depersonalized and disturbed and that mothers have been internalized "only as a source of frustration and anguish."[17] Duncan *et al.* in an analysis of homicidal males write of the "remorseless physical brutality" inflicted upon the subjects in childhood and adolescence by the parents.[18] Various research reports point to the anti-social nature of aggression releases pursued in early life by potentially assaultive and homicidal persons.[19] Cassity's study of 200 homicidal offenders led him to conclude that their backgrounds were socially inadequate.[20] Patterson's intensive analysis of juvenile offenders leads him to report that they developed in disorganized and economically marginal homes.[21] In a study of 20 children who committed homicide, Banay writes that "the composite statistical picture of these offenders speaks of a preponderance of unfavorable factors in home life and in personal and family relationships."[22] Gillin, in his report on Wisconsin male homicidal offenders, writes that common to their life histories was an overall "experience in the home which produces a sense of inferiority and of economic, emotional or social insecurity."[28]

Homicidal offenders tend to have developed, then, in hostile, unreciprocating environments. High tension has characterized interaction between mother and son. This has been punctuated by periods of no interaction due to the mother's withdrawal. Offenders have manifested aggressive outbursts that in turn lead others to be aggressive. Above all, offenders have become practiced in escalating unreciprocity to excessive heights.

3. Role Models and High Tension

As noted earlier, in the black ghetto father figures are frequently absent from the family.[24] Boys grow up without sex role models close at hand. And it is among young adult males in the black ghettos that homicide rates are especially high.[25] There is a tendency for young adult males to be homicidal or assaultive fathers who are seldom at home.

Bacon, Child, and Barry found in a cross-cultural study that personal crime, largely of an assaultive nature, showed a significant positive correlation with dependence socialization anxiety and with prolonged arrangements wherein mother and child slept together. They found that personal crime was positively associated with lack of opportunity for the young boy to form an identification with his father.[26] And Patterson reports that a major characteristic of homicidal juveniles is "mother attachment and father hatred."[27]

In the New England study, the fathers were usually living at home during the early lives of the offenders.[28] However, they were distinctly passive men. They deferred grudgingly to the mothers who were quite definitely the dominant figures in the family. Thus the offenders grew up with weak male images to emulate.[29] At the same time, the mothers insisted that their sons, the potential offenders, act with much decorum, almost with feminine comportment. They were more adamant about this in regard to offenders than to control brothers. As indicated above, mothers and offenders were locked into aggressive encounters; mothers used insistence on decorum by offenders as a veiled form of aggression.

Offenders thereby experienced extreme insecurity about the male role on two counts: the absence in the home of strong male models; and the presence of dominating mothers who threatened whatever sense of masculinity the offenders were able to develop. Tangible consequences were that offenders dated and married less often than either the control brothers or other adolescent and young adult males.[30]

The New England offenders, other groups of homicidal offenders, and growing males in the black ghettos have all experienced a related phenomenon of importance: Opportunities to learn various kinds of roles prized in the society at large have been severely limited. Opportunities to learn illegitimate roles have also been few. In the lower class environments of the potential homicidal offender there is simply a paucity of role models whom the boy can emulate.[31]

It is only slight exaggeration to say that the growing boy can emulate the older boy who hangs out on the street corner and few others. He can, it is true, turn to television and motion pictures for models. And he does. There he often finds roles that are gross caricatures of persons in everyday life, roles impossible of attainment.

Because of early life frustration, the unreciprocity of others and the lack of role models, the potential offender has had little opportunity to learn to perform roles adequately. He has not learned how to reciprocate but he has learned how to act with unreciprocity. As a consequence he is difficult toward others. Those others in turn act unreciprocatingly toward him, and they avoid him.

While others have not held especially high expectations for him, their expectations have nonetheless far outreached the potential offender's meager performances. And he has learned but few roles. He becomes an isolated loner, alienated from the mainstream of social life.[32] His inexperience in playing roles and his tendency to unreciprocating behavior are thereby compounded.

Both because of his inexperience and the unreciprocity of others, the potential offender's actual performances intefere with each other markedly. The time and energy required to perform one detract from the time and energy required for another. Having performed poorly and having had his performances judged as poor by others, the potential offender tends to perceive his performances as inadequate. He feels that it is exceedingly difficult to perform his roles. He finds that the performance of one role interferes with another greatly. As a consequence, tension in his inner system is high.[33]

As tension in the potential offender's inner system grows very great, explosion of that system threatens. The individual feels to a greater and greater degree pushed into a corner by the real and presumed exigencies of the various situations in which he finds himself. He views others with whom he interacts as blocking his attempts to ease interference among his performances.

There comes a time when he can tolerate no longer these circum-stances as he sees them. He erupts violently toward those, or toward surrogates for those, who seem to him to be his greatest frustraters.[34]

4. *The Lack of Identity*

Through the last several pages has run the implicit theme of identity—or the lack of it—in the lives of homicidal offenders. The concept is at once both imprecise and highly useful. Erikson writes of identity as "a subjective sense of an invigorating same-ness and continuity."[35] And later: "It is an active tension ... which furthermore must create a challenge 'without guarantee' rather than one dissipated by a clamor for certainty."[36]

Identity is a sense of recognition of the self-in-process. The individual is able to recognize himself in the mirror of his mind each morning. Yet he knows that he is forever changing. Identity can be seen as arising most readily from that state of the inner system in which tension is in the moderate range. The individual perceives his role performances as pulling against each other considerably but not overwhelmingly. His performances give form, albeit changing form, to his participation in everyday life. Performances, if tension with each other exists in moderate degree, provide the framework around which the social self exists.

If over the life history, however, tension in the inner system has been continually high, then it will have been exceedingly difficult for identity to coalesce. The individual will have per-ceived his performances as interfering with each other so greatly that there will have been little opportunity for the development of a coherent social self.

It is not difficult to see that the homicidal offender has been unable to fashion more than the shreds of identity. Ill, beaten, otherwise hurt as a child, unintegrated with his society, unable to learn adequately the sexual role, cut off from many other roles, his performances have been both poor and a burden for him. Whatever identity he has developed is largely negative: a picture of the self as one who is inadequate, whose lot it is to be frustrated.

People everywhere are vulnerable to "status threats," that is, to threats to whatever role playing ability they possess. The potential homicidal offender is especially vulnerable because his abilities here are so deficient. It is the unreciprocating slights to his masculinity that so often trigger violence. Any disparagement of masculinity is cause for the male to aggress, especially if he is of the lower class and black. He is expected to do so. And the subculture of violence is thus at hand, readily available. Both those expectations and that subculture have arisen in part because so many are so insecure about the male sexual role.[37]

The homicidal offender tends to be a highly uncertain person who feels perpetually backed to the wall. He has little power, little self-esteem, little security. He believes with some reason that others have pushed him too far for too long. When it appears to him that one or more threaten through unreciprocity to destroy whatever fragile identity he possesses, he takes violent action against them.

In the homicidal process, the offender creates for himself an identity. This blocked, insecure, powerless individual takes on momentarily great power. There is a large measure of certainty in his act. Having lived with little sense of self-recognition he becomes now for a short while the man of action, the man who controls his environment rather than being controlled by it. And while this sense of self is in some respects transitory, in others it is not. For as long as he exists, the homicidal offender will be known as one who has killed. Very likely he will be seen as such by others; in any event he will be so known to himself.[38]

5. *Delusion and the Masochistic Impulse*

The highly frustrated individual tends to become delusionary.[39] His life history has been a chain of experiences in which others appeared to him highly unpredictable. On many occasions others have failed to reciprocate, have been flatly unreciprocating and greatly frustrating. Yet those same individuals have been reciprocating and rewarding in many instances. For individuals to be unreciprocating all of the time verges on the impossible. Much of social life has built-in patterns of reciprocity and at least mild reward that are automatically followed.

The potential homicidal offender has a decided tendency to view others as alternating irrationally between reciprocity and unreciprocity. There seems to him to be no rhyme or reason to their "off-again on-again" behavior. (Many times he has had a small hope of reciprocity from others only to be bitterly disappointed.) When he was a child his mother in particular was in fact likely to behave in that way. In the early years, whether the mother reciprocated or unreciprocated toward him was often determined by her inner needs rather than by his behavior or by other conditions external to her.

As time went on, however, it is likely that there was a growing tendency for the actions of the offender's mother and of others to become geared to his actions. For reasons explained earlier, he will have become unreciprocating toward others. When he so acted, he will have triggered similar behavior by those others. But it is unlikely that he will have been aware of his part in the process. Seldom are individuals conscious of their own unreciprocity, particularly if they feel that others have mistreated them.

Both the actual and the seeming capriciousness of unreciprocity of other persons leads the individual to suspect the worst. He comes to magnify greatly that unreciprocity and the interference among his role performances that seem to be a consequence of it. To him that is the only safe course. Most or all others are from his standpoint dangerous. His suspicion gradually increases beyond that which is warranted by the facts of his existence and so turns to delusion. Delusion then becomes self-fulfilling prophecy.

The individual's ultradefensive, aggressive, suspicious posture structures the behavior of others such that when they respond they do so with increasing unreciprocity. But much of the time they do not respond; they avoid him. This leads to his partial exclusion from social life. It means that he will suffer in greater and greater degree from a lack of feedback from others. In such a socially sterile atmosphere, delusion is free to escalate rapidly to full-blown paranoia. As is well established, homicide rates for distinctly paranoidal persons are extremely high.[40]

Concurrent with the development of delusion, the potential offender is likely to become masochistic in the sense that he seeks unreciprocity and frustration from others.[41] He has lived a life of extreme frustration and he has survived. Thus frustration, particularly in the course of interaction, has come to be closely associated with, to stand for, life itself. That which represents life, survival, tends to be sought after. Hence the social masochism of the homicidal offender.[42]

The homicidal person becomes one, then, who gains a measure of reward out of the frustrating unreciprocity of those with whom he interacts. And to the extent that he can bring about their unreciprocity toward him, he validates his central thesis that they are "out to get" him. In this sense, delusion and masochism complement each other. Both arise out of frustration; each contributes to the growth of the other. The masochistic impulse furthers the delusionary view in its unwitting bid for frustration, for "persecution" by others. Delusions bring on that frustration by others which feeds on masochism. But only up to a point does the vicious circle spiral. Beyond a certain level, frustration by others will for the individual lose its masochistic component and be reconverted to sheer frustration. Then outward violence occurs.

Often it is the conjunction of situations or systems of situations in high tension and individuals with inner systems in high tension that provide the maximal conditions for homicide. Given situations where tension is exceedingly high, it will be those participants with highest inner tension who have the greatest likelihood of homicide.[43] That likelihood will be increased further and the precipitating spark set by sudden rises in the already high tension levels of both situational and inner systems. This is akin to strewing gasoline and lighted matches on parched forests.

6. *The Case of Nathan O'Brien*

Here is a case that illustrates various themes of this chapter.[44] Nathan O'Brien, eighteen, had been found "unruly" at the training school (reformatory) for boys and so was sent to the state prison. O'Brien was small, about five feet six inches tall and weighed 130 pounds, but was of athletic physique. His overall I.Q. was 120.

"Let's see," I said, "You first got in trouble when you were about fourteen and you were put on probation?"

"Yeah, another fellow and I were brought up for destroying property."

"What kind of property?"

"Cars, in a parking lot. We thought it was a junkyard."

"But did you really think that?"

"Looking at it now, no. But we convinced ourselves it was then." He spoke neither aggressively nor obsequiously.

"You were put on probation, but then a year or two later you were sent to the training school. Why was that?"

"Couple of other fellows and I pulled this job. We took a lot of clothes from a men's store."

"And you were in the training school what, about two years before you were sent here?"

"In and out."

"How many times did you escape?"

"Three."

"Why did you?"

"I didn't like it. I was kind of mad."

"Why were you mad?"

"This girl I'd been going with had a baby and I wanted to marry her."

"You were the father?"

"Yeah. And I asked the superintendent to let me marry her but he said I was crazy."

"When you escaped did you try to marry her?"

"I never got that far. I was picked up."

"What do you want to do when you leave here?" He was due to be released in four months.

"I've got this warrant hanging over me—for picking up a car. If I can get out of that I want to box."

"Fight professionally?"

"Yeah, a couple of guys have been coaching me in here. I've had a couple of fights but I need more training, a lot more."

In the prison he had fought in the ring several times and each time had been beaten badly. He had a reputation for wading in, being knocked out of the ring, going back in and bluffing that he would carry the fight to his opponent, then being knocked down or out again.

"I'd go down to this gym I know, Monello's. There's a guy there said he'd take me on, he'd manage me."

"And your aim is to become a famous fighter."

"Yeah."

"But you realize that the odds are one in a million. Even if you learn to fight well, extremely well, you have to have the right connections."

"I know but maybe I could make it."

"Is there anything else you'd like to do?"

"I'd like to be boss of this company, this furniture company, in Arlington."

"Is that where your father works?"

"Yeah. He's been there for twenty-five years."

"What does he do?"

"Drives a truck. That's all he's done for twenty-five years."

"How do you feel about your father? What do you think of him?"

"He's all right, I suppose. But he doesn't want to get anywhere. He doesn't have any drive, if you see what I mean. He's weak. Weak."

"And you'd like to be his boss?"

"Yeah. Well, not just that but—yeah, I suppose so."

"But do you really think you have any chance of being head of this furniture company some day?"

"No. No. I worked there a couple of times. I was the assistant dispatcher for a while in the summer. I was really my father's boss then. But I never could stick at it. But fighting, I could stick at that."

"What you want to do is put all your eggs in one basket—make fighting, getting somewhere at that, your one goal."

"Yeah."

"Do you have any interest in going further in education, in school?"

"No, I couldn't," O'Brien answered. "In the training school I took these courses, I finished three years of high school."

"How were your grades?"

"Pretty high. A's and B's."

"You could probably finish high school quickly, in a summer course say, and you could probably be accepted in a college."

"No—how do they feel about somebody with a record in college?"

"It doesn't matter. At least in many colleges, it doesn't make any difference."

"I couldn't do it."

"Why?"

"I'm kind of funny about that. Education, going to school, getting a job. I can't do things like that. I feel, I get, well, embarrassed. Like when I go somewhere to get a job, the guy asks me what I can do and I tell him I can do the job all right. But they ask me what experience I've got, just what can I do and I can't tell them. I just can't say anything, I feel embarrassed and like I'm begging, and I don't get the job."

"What do you think is the main reason that you've gotten in trouble with the law. What do you think has been the central reason you've been motivated to violate the law?"

He thought. "I don't know. I think it's—well, you sit around with a couple of fellows you know and you have a few drinks and you feel better. And they want to do something, pull a job, and you want to do it with them, you feel good, you feel you're in a group. That's it, it's that I feel I'm part of a group."

"But how do you feel otherwise, say when you're by yourself, before you sit around with a few friends and drink?"

"Well, kind of nervous. Jumpy. Alone."

"Do you feel angry toward people very much?"

"No. I think it's wrong to do that."

"How do you feel about the other men in the prison here? What are they like in general?"

"The trouble with them is, they're lazy, they want a shortcut to everything, they think they're too good to work."

"What about you? Do you feel that you're much like them?"

"Yeah, that's it. I'm the same way."

"What's the first thing in life that you remember?"

"Oh—it was my birthday. My fifth birthday. I fell off the porch."

"Were you hurt?"

"Yeah. It was a second floor porch. The second floor was set back from the front and there was a porch there, open, with a railing around it. They had this party for my birthday and I backed up and I went over the railing. I landed on my head. I was knocked out. My father took me to the hospital. In a few days I was all right."

"How did your father act toward you when you were young?"

"He didn't pay much attention. We never did anything. I wanted to go to baseball games and things but he never would. He drank a lot but he always went to work. I'll say that."

"What was your mother like when you were young? How did she act toward you?"

"I don't know. She was kind of quiet. She was sick a lot. She always worked, though."

"What did she do?"

"Waitress."

"What other incidents in your childhood stand out clearly in your mind?"

"I burned the house down."

"How did that happen? How old were you?"

"I was seven. This other kid—in the neighborhood—and I were alone in the house. They had this paint and turpentine or something around. We were fooling around with the matches and I threw one in there. I didn't think it would burn. But it did, curtains got on fire, and then the whole thing was going."

"What happened then?"

"They got the firetrucks but it was too late. My mother and father came home and they were watching it. I called them over and I told them I started it."

"What did they do?"

"Oh, they got mad, my mother was crying. They kind of got over it but any time after that if I was going to do anything they'd bring that up and tell me I was no good and that I couldn't do things like other kids because I was different, because of the fire."

"What did—" I started to ask.

O'Brien interrupted. "The trouble with me is, I'm kind of funny. It's like I didn't have any personality, like something's missing. I told you, I can't get a job, I feel like there's nothing there, inside me."

"What do you want most in the world?"

There was a long pause.

"Security."

"How do you feel about the future, do you think there's much chance that you'll go straight after you leave here?"

"No, I don't know what it is. I want to. I want to be—well, decent, good. But I don't think so. I—I know it won't work out like that."

A short time later O'Brien was released from the state prison, detained immediately afterwards in a local jail to await trial on the car theft charge. He beat a jail guard to death and escaped. He went seventy miles to a large city, hid out for two weeks. Then he returned to his home town of Arlington, hid out again, this time in a rooming house a few doors down the street from the police station. He was soon apprehended, brought to trial, sentenced to thirty to forty years imprisonment.

O'Brien's father came to the prison to see him. The father was highly intoxicated, but in the Sunday press of visitors this escaped the attention of the guards at the main gate. The father went into the ladies' room in the prison, caused an extended commotion, and was finally removed without seeing his son.

CHAPTER IV

The Social Control of Homicide

1. *The Absence of Prevention*

This chapter is devoted to certain of the myriad interrelationships between the social control process and homicidal behavior in the United States. The considerable lack of national concern with the prevention of homicide is discussed. The process by which individuals are labeled as homicidal is emphasized. So too are the processes by which sanctions are brought to bear against those labeled by police, courts, and prisons. Some similarities between control agents and offenders are traced. The social uses of homicide are considered. Finally, attention is given to ways by which the society might increase the effectiveness of its social control regarding homicide.

One of the most striking facts about the social control process in relation to homicide and to crime in general in this and many other societies is the clear lack of emphasis on preventive measures.[1] It would be difficult consciously to design a system that took prevention so little into account. Yet the indicators of high probabilities of homicide are quite clear. As discussed earlier, when a group internalizes the success goals of the larger society and is then denied access to the means for achieving those goals, that is, when competition is excessive, outward violence is to be expected.

Certainly, there are difficulties in predicting which particular individuals will commit homicide.[2] This is in part because one must be able to predict the situations in which individuals will be involved. At the same time, characteristics of potentially violent persons are fairly well established: As noted earlier, they have suffered severe, prolonged frustration of various types in early life. They find great difficulty in carrying out their role obligations. They are highly resentful and suspicious. They are as a rule withdrawn persons whose quiet demeanor is sporad-

67

ically punctuated by aggressive outbursts against other persons or animals. Further, they are either unable to fit into the confines of routinized situations such as those that may be found at school and work or they find refuge in excessive involvement in such routine.[3]

If mechanisms were established for identifying children, adolescents, and young adults who show such characteristics in the extreme, several outcomes might obtain:[4] Treatment could be provided through appropriate forms of psychotherapy and "group relations" therapy. (The latter may involve the taking on of new roles, the shedding of old roles, and so on.) Alternately, individuals could be labeled as potential homicidal offenders and no treatment made available. The effects of such labeling could well be self-prophetic.[5] Again, some combination of labeling and treatment might obtain. Here treatment might be designed to obviate the negative effects of labeling as well as to create non-homicidal conditions within the individuals so designated and within their environments as well.

However, in practice the control process in the United States operates in response to the commission of criminal homicide rather than in anticipation of potential homicide, rather, that is, than as a preventive force. At times, and as will be documented, the control process serves to induce the problem it is ostensibly designed to reduce, a not uncommon outcome in the affairs of men.

2. The Labeling Process

When highly frustrated children follow a pattern of occasionally bursting out with aggressive acts and otherwise withdraw from the world around them, other individuals have a tendency to label them as peculiar. As reported in the previous chapter, "You are not like other children," was a refrain used by Nathan O'Brien's parents when he, at age seven, burned down their house. "There's something wrong with him" and "he's different" are common responses to children who from time to time burst forth with violence. By middle adolescence, it is extremely likely that within whatever weak identity such a child possesses the image of himself as an unaccepted outsider will be strong.[6]

While most homicides are reported by persons other than the police,[7] it is the police who are expected first to label the individual as homicidal. They arrest him, book him, hold him for a preliminary hearing. If the evidence is more than minimal, and occasionally when it is minimal, the police are likely to act as if the suspect were guilty. While the legal philosophy is otherwise, in practice the accused tends to be treated as guilty from time of arrest until the court verdict. The burden is in fact upon him to demonstrate his innocence.[8]

The prosecution is likely to label the defendant in a criminal homicide trial as a figure to be abhorred in the extreme: "a miserable misfit who has perpetrated this heinous crime" and so on. Trial court judges are not always averse to labeling the offender, at the time of sentencing, as, for example, "a menace to society" who has "forfeited the right to membership in the human race." Newspaper, television, radio, and other mass media provide the bases for almost instantaneous and exceedingly widespread labeling of suspects. While they do not directly point to him as guilty, they do tend by clear implication to label the accused as a violent offender: "A man who fits the description of 'the mad strangler.'"

In prison, the homicidal offender is not treated as "a dime-a-dozen" pickpocket. He enters with the status and role of "lifer" or "long-termer" and with at least a vaguely discernible "rep" already established because of his crime. He is special. Other things equal, he will rise in the power-prestige hierarchy of the prison more quickly than those convicted of most other crimes.[9]

If after ten to twenty or more years of imprisonment he is paroled or conditionally pardoned, the label of one who has committed homicide goes with the released man.[10] The parole or pardon board considers essentially the question of whether this individual who has been convicted of criminal homicide will recommit the crime. The members of the board may discuss the likelihood of this with him. When they do not, other inmates will make clear to him that this is the question uppermost in the board's deliberation. If the decision is not to parole or pardon him, then the individual is aware that he is judged to be a prospect for further homicidal behavior. If he is paroled or pardoned, he knows he is seen by board members as an ex-homicidal offender who is now considered "safe." In either case, the mass media intensify the labeling process.

When he is out in the wider community, the discharged individual is likely to be seen as an "ex-lifer," as one who committed murder at some past time. In sum, from arrest until death, the offender is known as one who has killed. If in certain instances others do not know, then the individual is acutely aware that they do not and that they may come to know at some future time.

In those instances when the homicidal offender is executed, he is likely first to have spent several years on "death row."[11] He is known as one who is to "suffer the supreme penalty" for what is considered the most extremely negative act against his society, for breaching one of the society's most serious strictures. He "pays with his life" for having "taken a life."

While labeling often directly serves to beget the behavior it designates, the process in regard to homicide is more complex. Labeling in early life as peculiar and the like may of course to some degree move an individual toward homicide. However, the more usual use of labeling here is that it makes possible a potential identity which can be achieved through killing one or more others. The individual knows that if he commits homicide he will be labeled as a "murderer" and in that sense will gain an identity.

In any event, the labeling process is likely to be rewarding both to those who are labeled and to those who do the labeling. For the offender the reward value of a place in the municipal, regional, or national spotlight may be very great. After all, it is only those persons considered as exceptional in some way who are spotlighted. To many who have received no recognition by the society, a picture in the paper, a short sequence on television, can be the highpoints of a barren life career regardless of why the individual is news.

Further, such labeling provides the offender with a clear identity that he may well never have experienced previously. To be sure, it is in many respects a negative identity from the standpoint of the society's value system. However, labeling as one who has killed connotes to many a person of action and power. And there are not a few members of the society who have only partially hidden admiration for the violent offender. Everything considered, for those who are blocked from achieving socially approved identities, the labels and the statuses and the roles of "killer" and "ex-killer" may be far more rewarding than nothing.

Some reward may accrue to the labelers as well. Police, prosecutor, judge, parole board member, everyday citizen may gain a certain stature in the community by their vigorous denunciation of the accused or convicted person. Righteous indignation set forth against offenders by the various agents of control begets a measure of applause from the general public. And it is not to be overlooked that those who officially represent the society in its quest for the designation of the outwardly violent deviant may gain a certain inner satisfaction as spokesman of "justice." Further such fringe benefits of the failure to control homicide are discussed toward the end of this chapter.

3. *Conviction*

The rewards that may occur to offenders by being placed in the social spotlight and by the acquiring of an identity, however negative, have just been discussed. The punishments, informal and formal, set forth by the police, the courts, and the prisons are numerous and diverse and it is to them that the discussion now turns. Use by police of "third-degree" methods to extort confessions of homicidal suspects is far from uncommon.[12] On the other hand, in the ghetto and on skid row, the police more than occasionally look the other way when homicide occurs and thus fail to initiate the sanctioning process.[13] Detention prior to trial serves as a punishment to many accused persons whether or not they are guilty. Often the accused is held in jail from six months to a year before the trial begins.[14]

The judicial system in this and many other societies operates on an erroneous hedonistic psychology in regard to homicide and other criminal cases.[15] It is assumed that all persons receive the same amount of satisfaction from the commission of homicide. It is also assumed that the deterrent value of a certain degree of punishment will be the same for all persons. The aim is to set the punishment so that its frustration value slightly outweighs the reward value of the crime. This is the heart of the criminal control system in the United States. On this basis alone the widespread ineffectiveness of that system is to be expected.[16]

As is well known, justice in the United States varies by race. In his study of Philadelphia homicides, Wolfgang found that of those 409 blacks who stood trial, 81 per cent were found guilty. Of 117 whites tried, 62 per cent were convicted.[17] Reporting on a second study, of 500 individuals who were to be executed, Wolfgang states that of 147 blacks to be executed, the sentences of 11.6 per cent were commuted; of 263 whites, the sentences of 20.2 per cent were commuted. It is sometimes said that blacks are executed more frequently than whites proportional to numbers because they tend more than whites to commit criminal homicide in connection with the perpetration of another felony. When felony-murders only were analyzed, Wolfgang's results showed that sentences of 6.3 per cent of blacks were commuted; almost three times as many whites, 17.4 per cent, had their sentences commuted.[18]

In an analysis of 821 southern homicides, Garfinkel found the following:[19] Of those cases where the offender was black and the victim white, 80 per cent of offenders were convicted; where both offender and victim were white, 62 per cent were convicted; where both were black, 77 per cent were convicted; and where the offender was white and the victim black, 63 per cent were convicted. Convictions for first-degree murder were greatest by far when the offender was black and the victim white. Of all such cases, 29 per cent of offenders were found guilty of first degree murder. In contrast, of those cases where offender was white and victim black, none was convicted of first-degree murder. Of those where offender and victim were both white, seven per cent were found guilty of murder in the first-degree; where offenders and victims were both black, the figure was three per cent.

Mistakes in verdicts in criminal homicide trials are less uncommon than many suppose. Lewis Lawes and Frank Hartung have each indicated that of groups of persons convicted of homicide and studied by them about 10 per cent were later found to be innocent.[20] Since motivation to exonerate a dead man or one who has served many years in prison is not great and since it is exceedingly difficult to demonstrate innocence once an individual has been found guilty, the figure may well be considerably above 10 per cent. Certainly there is a strong tendency in the society and therefore among the society's agents of control—police, prosecutors and judiciary—to designate some-one as responsible for a given homicidal crime.[21] And seldom are routine procedures available for releasing and indemnifying those wrongly convicted.[22] Usually new laws must be passed. An innocent person who has served a number of years in prison may be compensated by a sum of money or he may receive nothing.

4. *Imprisonment*

At the time of sentencing for homicide, most offenders have not previously been inmates in a prison.[23] And, obvious as it may be, none has been executed. Their experience as to the meaning of such punishments is therefore very limited. The prison environment turns out for many inmates to be a highly complex mixture of frustration and reward. Sykes writes with much insight of the "pains of imprisonment."[24] He points to the deprivation of liberty due both to confinement to the institution and to restriction to certain places within the institution. Relatedly, Sykes notes the deprivation of autonomy: in addition to sheer confinement the inmate's choices in many realms of life are severely limited. He writes of the deprivation of goods and services, especially of the symbols of existence beyond the sheer subsistence level. There is, further, the severe deprivation of heterosexual relationships.

Finally, Sykes discusses the deprivation of security. Prison is for many an insecure environment, physically as well as psycho-logically. Where assault will break out is never certain from the inmate's standpoint. And as Sykes says, at some point the inmate will be tested to see whether or not he will fight for his rights. If he fails, he will be an "object of contempt, constantly in danger of being attacked."[25] If he succeeds, he is likely to become a prime target for other inmates who seek to prove themselves. "Thus both success and failure in defending one's self against the aggressions of fellow captives may serve to provoke fresh attacks and no man stands assured of the future."[26] Further, there remains the threat and the fact of negative sanctions imposed by prison administrative personnel. Solitary confinement is used as the warden or his deputy deems necessary. Brutality by guards is still a fact of prison life.[27] And the death of inmates who in some fashion run afoul of administrators' wishes is far from unknown.[28]

However, prison is also an opportunity structure that can be rewarding to inmates. The very lack of liberty and autonomy, the routinization of life, provide a stable, secure environment for some individuals. For those highly insecure about their sex role, the absence of possibilities for heterosexual relationships, and the absence of expectations for those relationships, may be distinctly rewarding. And there is evidence that for many this is so.[29] Perhaps paramount, the world of the prison is a place where a man who could not succeed elsewhere may have one further choice for success.[30] To build a real leadership role in the prison society and to gain prestige as a leader among men who have seriously transgressed the society's mores, are not lightly to be dismissed.

Further, for those of strong masochistic persuasion, the earlier mentioned pains of imprisonment may take on a positive coloration. The brutality of guards, the isolation of solitary confinement, the hampering restrictions, the social stigma of incarceration, the denial of companions of the other sex can all be highly rewarding for individuals who have come through earlier experience to associate degradation and pain with life itself, with survival.

As is well known, prisons are extremely limited in regard to formally devised rehabilitative facilities. Little individual or group therapy occurs in prison. State legislatures provide funds for the general functioning of the prison, for maintaining the prison industries, and for insuring that inmates do not escape. But they seldom provide anything approaching substantial funds for rehabilitation.[31] Yet homicidal offenders have high success rates upon release from prison; that is, they seldom return to prison.[32] They are extremely unlikely to recommit homicide.[33] One study found that first degree murder offenders had less probability of violating parole than those convicted of any other felony.[34] Further, only two per cent of offenders found guilty of first degree murder were subsequently convicted of a felony as compared to 4.7 per cent of second degree murderers; 8.1 per cent of rapists; 21.8 per cent of robbers; 17.4 per cent of grand larcenists; 30.2 per cent of forgers; and 31.1 per cent of automobile thieves.[35]

To what extent the daily life of prison, disagreeable as it appears to the outsider, may be implicitly conducive to the rehabilitation of homicidal persons is unknown. The above data make it clear that prisons do not show much tendency to induce homicide. In any event it is useful to bear in mind the difficulty of gaining admission to state or federal prisons in the United States. Taken together, those institutions can house only two to three hundred thousand inmates.[36] Most convicted felons are housed in local jails or are placed on probation.[37] If some individuals have needs for the identity and for the routinization and the pains that may be consequences of imprisonment, the commission of homicide insures fulfillment of those needs more effectively than most other deviant acts: Long-term access to prison opportunity structures and to the status and role of inmate is facilitated for homicidal offenders.

5. Execution

As has been pointed out on numerous occasions, the processes of deviance and of the mechanisms designed to control it are often mirror images of each other.[38] So it has been in some respects regarding homicidal violence and its control: Killing is met with killing. Since 1930 in the United States between 4000 and 5000 persons have been legally executed. Electrocuting, hanging, gassing and shooting of offenders have been the methods. Sellin summarizes the major forms of execution in the United States in recent times: "Twenty-one states and the District of Columbia used electric chairs in 1930, one used lethal gas (Nevada), one gave the prisoner a choice between hanging or a firing squad (Utah), one used electrocution or, if the crime was rape, hanging (Kentucky), and 17 states and the Federal prisons used gallows. By 1965, considerable changes had occurred. Twenty-four states had installed electric chairs, eleven had gas chambers, and seven had gallows. No change had been made in Utah. . . . When Oregon, Iowa and West Virginia became abolitionist states in 1965, the number of electric chairs, gas chambers and gallows was reduced by one each."[39]

Faulty procedures, resulting in slow death, have been common. Hangings are regularly botched so that the victim slowly strangles or is cut down and hanged again.[40] Electrocutions have not been without difficulty. Elliott, the chief executioner at Sing Sing prison for many years, recalls one instance where a supposedly executed man was discovered moving in the prison morgue. Upon being strapped in the electric chair once again, the condemned man died of a heart attack.[41] (See case at end of this chapter.)

If private individuals were to electrocute, or half-electrocute, another person, they would be thought guilty of a particularly heinous crime. So would they if they were to hang someone, perhaps decapitating the victim in the process, as occasionally occurs in state-sanctioned death. Gassing others and the use of firing squads would be similarly construed by the society at large.

Legislative vestiges of the death penalty are worthy of note. A number of states retain execution for treason, although treason against a particular state is no longer a reality. New York retains the death penalty for the killing of a police officer on duty or of a prison guard by an inmate previously sentenced to life imprisonment for criminal homicide.[42] On the other hand, Michigan abolished capital punishment for treason in 1963. Delaware abolished the death penalty in 1957 and restored it for homicide in 1961.[43]

In any case, the legalized killing of others, the use of execution as a social control response to homicide, has decreased in recent years both in and out of the United States. African and North American countries in general retain the death penalty.[44]

Many Latin American countries have abolished it. So have most European countries. Among Western European countries only France, Ireland, and Turkey still use capital punishment for homicide.[45] In the United States, there were in 1930 eight abolitionist states; now there are 13.[46]

During the 1930's in the United States, 167 individuals were executed each year on the average. In the 1940's, the figure was 128; during the 1950's, 72. The annual average for the years 1960-65 was 32.[47] And in 1968 there were no executions in this country. However, in that year over 500 prisoners were on "death-row," awaiting execution. Of 3856 civil executions over the years from 1930 through 1965, the vast majority, 3362, were for murder; 455 were for rape and 69 for other offenses. About half of those executed during that period were blacks. And but 0.9 per cent were females.[48]

The decline in legalized killing may signal a basic change in the societal outlook on violence.[49] It may very well be that once a society is able to reduce such killing significantly it is on its way to gradual reduction of illegal killing. Put differently, if execution by the state is directly symptomatic of underlying social forces that generate violence, then a reduction in executions may be possible only as a consequence of a decrease in those forces. Since there probably is a lead time here of several decades, we are unlikely in the near future to have solid evidence on this as it pertains to the United States.

6. *Similarities Between Offenders and Agents of Control*

Similarities between deviants and the agents assigned by society to control them have also been noted from time to time. Executioners have shown something of an affinity for dying on the gallows or being otherwise punished for committing homicide.[50] MacDonald reports on a number of English hangmen later convicted of murder.[51] A reverse instance is that of a man who was to be executed for horse stealing in the England of Charles II. His father and older brothers had been convicted of the same crime and sentenced also to execution. The bench of judges ruled they would pardon any one of the three who agreed to hang the other two. The younger son agreed and carried out efficiently his part of the bargain. He was later appointed official hangman for Derby and the surrounding counties and made a considerable career in that capacity.[52]

Brutality by prison guards and administrators often at the least matches that of homicidal and assaultive offenders. Documentation of persistent violence by prison personnel is sufficiently extensive to demonstrate this.[53] The number of homicides in prison is not insignificant. Guards and inmates are subject to many of the same environmental conditions. Guards on occasion go "stir-crazy." Over the years they tend to internalize inmate values.[54]

As has been noted, police may act assaultively toward suspects. In recent times, an increasing amount of homicide by police "in the line of duty" has been demonstrated to be illegal. The shooting and killing by police of innocent bystanders, often children, during rioting and looting episodes are coming to light. Victims tend to be black. The President's Commission on Civil Rights documents such cases in which police have killed those whom they have arrested on minimal or fabricated evidence.[55]

Just as homicidal offenders may gain a certain sense of identity from the control process, so may agents of that process by virtue of their involvement in it. The role of the police officer provides an identity as a powerful defender of "law and order." In a highly localized sense, police do wield much power. They are expected to take action against those who would seem to threaten the prevailing political system. While occasionally they are instructed otherwise, as a rule police are expected to arrest those who appear to be, or are, rioting and looting.[56] If a person inadvertently or otherwise defies arrest, many hold expectations that the police officer should shoot him.

The prison guard is in a position to take on a special identity. He at least ostensibly controls men who have demonstrated that they are serious violators of the criminal law. He holds a secure niche in the machinery of protecting society's members from wrong-doers. He stands between inmates and that liberty which would allow them to kill, assault, or steal. While he may at times enter into deals with inmates, he nonetheless can take on the identity as protector of safe sleep of citizens everywhere.[57] Moreover, executioners are charged with killing in the name of the state and nothing else. They are sanctified killers. Prosecutors are charged with seeing that the guilty are convicted. Trial judges, clearly the most prestigious of the various agents of control, must above all see that "justice is done," that punishment is meted out. The control process has the social use, then, of providing some degree of identity for a wide array of persons.

7. *The Social Uses of Homicide*

There will be further social uses of homicide and its control, some of which are related to the possibilities of gaining identity that have just been discussed. Tension in the inner role system of the individual is likely to decrease to a degree once the homicidal act is carried out. Not only may decisive action, violent action, have been taken against one or more of those whom the offender has viewed as making the performance of his roles exceedingly difficult. Once apprehended, the number of his roles is automatically reduced considerably. If he has been playing husband, father and occupational roles, and if they have been difficult for him, then he need play them no longer, His main role is that of homicidal offender, of "inmate-who-has-killed-somebody." Over the years the role of homicidal inmate is central to the inner system. Because he has few roles and because the homicidal role overshadows other remaining roles, interference among the individual's performances tends to be less and to be perceived by him as less than prior to apprehension. Thus tension in the inner system is likely to be lower than previously.[58]

In certain respects, the offender is provided with a degree of integration into his society that he did not have prior to his violence. The role of homicidal persons links him, binds him, to his society despite the popular belief that the long-term inmate is a social outcast. His explosion of power that leads to the death of another is met with a highly ambivalent response by the larger society. He is in part loathed and in part secretly admired. He is the despised hero, a role that can only exist in relation to the society as a whole. Moreover, the societal expectations for him in the inmate role and his actual performance in that role are likely to be rather well aligned. Thus, through the outer role of homicidal inmate a definite linkage between the offender and his society is forged.

A further use of homicide, and of other serious crimes as well, and an important one, is that it serves, through the social control apparatus that develops, to institutionalize violence as a legitimate social response. There is a certain self-righteous quality that permeates patterns of police and guard brutality and of execution. The society is provided with rationalized revenge. In allowing and in fact requiring the expression of severe aggression toward others, the occupations of police officer and guard make possible two widespread roles wherein individuals can behave violently in more or less socially acceptable and "orderly" fashion.

Durkheim wrote of crime as a means of engendering social organization.[59] To some degree, at least, the members of the society at large band together against the criminal, the "outlaw," wreak vengeance upon him and in so doing develop solidarity. Relatedly, Kai Erikson has provided in his *Wayward Puritans* a faithful picture of the ways in which a group maintains its boundaries, its identity, through the intricate process of creating heretical deviants.[60] Homicidal offenders by their violence mark the outer limits of social unacceptability. They are "killers" and other men are not. The vast majority, some of whom may themselves have homicidal tendencies, are by contrast identified as men of peace.

Coser selects for special analysis three social uses of violence.[61] The first of these is achievement. Those who are blocked from goal-attainments of the types common in the society may turn to violence as a form of achievement. This has in effect already been considered at some length in regard to the search for identity. Secondly, Coser suggests that violence can serve as a social warning, a danger signal. As tensions in the society mount to severely high levels, violence that takes homicidal and other forms breaks out, signaling present or future social disorganization. "This signal is so drastic, so extremely loud," Coser writes, "that it can not fail to be perceived by men in power and authority otherwise not noted for peculiar sensitivity to social ills."[62]

To extend Coser's view, there is a related and yet in a sense opposite consequence of homicide. An annual homicide rate of 10 per 100,000 of the population is extremely high but it does not indicate a mass phenomenon in the usual sense. That is, if in a society of one hundred million people, ten thousand are homicide victims annually, the society is unlikely to be construed sociologically as one that is torn by violence the way, say, the United States was during the Civil War. The point is this: homicide may serve as an alternative to internal war, to a greater bloodshed, while it also is indicative of undue tension in the society.

Coser refers to a third use. Violence can act as a catalyst for social change. He notes the violence of southern police in racial confrontations. Police brutality against those engaged in non-violent protest activities catalyzed public opinion to some extent and resulted both in new federal legislation and in greater enforcement of existing legislation. Similarly, it should be added, homicide by police against young and innocent blacks forces upon the national attention the necessity of improving life in the ghetto. In parallel fashion, it can be the violence of homicidal offenders (non-police) that precipitates change. Depending on a variety of related factors, homicide emanating from a particular group certainly may bring forth change in the form of greater retaliation, stronger negative sanctions, than previously obtained. However, it may, functioning as the signaling mechanism just mentioned, lead to the opposite response, to a decrease in the tension level of the social environment of the group which manifests the homicide.

Finally, this should be noted: The crime control apparatus in the United States, as it applies to the total span of felonies and misdemeanors, is a vast enterprise. It is big business. It provides employment, some highly prestigious and much not, for hundreds of thousands of persons. There are over 200,000 men and women employed in 40,000 public law enforcement agencies in the United States. The cost of maintaining these agencies exceeds one billion dollars annually.[63] Each year more than a million persons are admitted to 10,000 county and city jails and other local places of enforced confinement.[64] Well over 200,000 inmates are housed in state and federal prisons in the United States,[65] most of them in the 130 major state prisons.[66] Thousands of judges, probation and parole officers, and hundreds of thousands of prison and jail administrative and guard personnel are employed full-time by the crime control apparatus.

Thus criminal deviance supports a wide span of workers and facilities in the society. The control of homicidal violence is a spearhead of this vast enterprise. Most sizable police departments have their homicide squads. Murder trials involve numerous highly trained people. Lawyers specialize in defending those accused of capital crimes. Prisons are "maximum security" institutions in order to prevent the escape of those convicted of murder, manslaughter, and other serious crimes. Many state prisons have their "death row." And while the role of executioner has in considerable part passed from the scene, gallows, electric chairs and gas chambers are still maintained in operating order.

When homicide occurs in greater numbers than usual, alarm spreads through the society.[67] There is an underlying belief that if murder and manslaughter cannot be controlled, then social organization is on the brink of disaster. At the same time, the social uses outlined above are served by both homicidal behavior and the attempts to control it. As is plain to see, if the control apparatus were highly effective, those social uses would be largely negated and agents of control would put themselves out of business.

What the members of society believe they want are the manifest purposes of control while what they may actually want are the latent uses of deviance. If social control enterprises are to exist and expand, the agents of control must accomplish two things. They must so comport themselves that they seem to make a genuine effort to give the society the kind of effective control its members loudly proclaim they desire. Simultaneously, they must in fact provide that ineffective control that allows the silent, unconscious needs of the populace to be well met.

8. Effective Controls

From the standpoint of the theoretical formulation set forth here, the effective control of homicide ultimately depends in large measure upon two related conditions: the reduction of tension in social systems and situations and in the inner status and role systems of individuals to something less than extremely high levels; and the avoidance of abrupt large-scale increases in tensions of those. How to accomplish these ends is exceedingly difficult for numerous reasons. Not the least is simple inertia of many of the society's members. While high tension can be greatly frustrating, it may be all the members of the society know. Seldom is the unknown preferable to the known. As will be demonstrated at a later point, the unknown prospects of low tension in inner or social systems are especially terrorizing to many. Further, the social uses of homicide just discussed would be rendered increasingly unavailable if the control of homicide were gradually to become effective. The society's members are unlikely to relinquish those uses readily.

As previously stated, if children with homicidal tendencies were singled out for treatment, there would be the danger of the self-fulfilling aspects of so labeling them. At the same time, they are in any case labeled informally as peculiar. Further, these are children who have been so hurt that the necessity for treatment is highly urgent. But what form of treatment?

To decrease tension in the child's inner system requires a steady flow of moderate reciprocity from others. Very gradually the hurt child comes to perceive that it is less difficult to do what he must than was the case previously. Slowly he begins to see that this happens because others help him more and impede him less. He tests those others to see if they really mean to help him: He refuses to reciprocate and waits to find out what will happen. If the others revert to their old stand of unreciprocity all is lost insofar as treatment goes. If they persist in their new approach to him, he tries tentatively petty moves of reciprocity toward them. This signals that for better or for worse he is now on his way into the mainstream of his society.

What is important in treatment is the posture by others of some moderate degree of reciprocity toward the violent child and particularly as that reciprocity is sustained during his altogether necessary testing of them. It means the beginning of identity for him as one who is related by interaction to someone else. It marks a downturn in his previously upwardly spiraling delusions; for automatic suspicion of others is for him no longer an absolute necessity.

But how to insure that the social systems in which the child will move from this point forward are in less than great tension and will not be characterized by large upward swings of tension? Connect him to persons who participate in such social systems, in social systems not in high tension. He must have the opportunities to take on roles in those systems. Opportunities to revert to the old roles in high tension social systems must be closed off. That this is unlikely to happen in practice demonstrates the basic problem: There are in the United States many situations and social systems in high tension and few in moderate tension. The latter have a long waiting line.

One might argue that the latent functions of violence are indispensable for social organization and that violence must therefore be tolerated. That may be. At the same time it may be less than unreasonable to attempt to determine whether or not action taken broadly in the society can cause some of the killing to stop and yet leave the society still standing.

As is so often the case with attempts at social control, the great danger is that whatever controlling action is taken will worsen rather than ease the problem. The danger in the present instance is that the prevailing high tension conditions will be exacerbated rather than ameliorated. Usually, to be effective controls must be exerted with a light touch or resistance to them mounts. Sometimes, but not always, no action may be the most effective form of control. When violence is most imminent, often the best thing will be to do nothing. Any action is likely to be construed by participants as a further example of unreciprocity and so may trigger more violence than would otherwise have resulted. As has so often been noted there are an ebb and flow in human affairs and this applies to tension in social systems. Even though tension in a given system may be habitually great, it will drift back and forth between very high and somewhat less high levels.

The matter can be put this way: Social control is usually most effective in making inroads on the problem at hand when it seems to participants to be needed least.[68] When tension in a

social system has subsided to some degree and violence is on the
wane, this is the time to bring controls to bear. It has been
suggested here that innovation is most likely when tension in a
social system is in the moderate range. Thus the most propitious
time for introducing innovation into a social system characterized
by great tension occurs when that tension has abated to whatever
extent it will abate (although in absolute terms tension may still
be quite high).

A little bit of innovation goes a long way. Large amounts of it
are threatening to participants in whatever kinds of social
systems because the *status quo* is radically disorganized. Small
amounts are rewarding for they provide without significant disorganization a glimpse of the benefits to be gained from expressing oneself in ways that lead to new problem solutions.

At those times when tension in a social system is less high than
usual, the aim of social control should be to allow participants to
hit upon alternative solutions to the problems of how to reverse
rising tension in the social system and in the inner systems as
well. There are other ways of coping with mounting tension than
to snowball unreciprocity into violence. Individuals can learn to
verbalize their hostilities toward one another in situations agreed
upon by them as ones designed for that purpose.[69] They can
employ their pooled energies to redirect the social wellsprings of
high tension. They can embark upon projects of adventure and
discovery that absorb the restlessness and free-floating aggression of those grown accustomed to high tension and fearful of
low tension. Involvement in new lines of political activity such
as the 1968 young people's crusade for the candidacy of Eugene
McCarthy for President is an illustration. What all this means at
basis is that new forms of competition must be devised, political
and otherwise, wherein participants do in fact from time to time
have a fairly good chance of winning.

In the urban core, a major possibility is the involvement of
violent youth in the one broad aspect of the political realm:
their participation in federally financed community action programs.[70] Here are opportunities for alienated youth to experi-
ment with the social environment, make over as innovatively as
possible the social systems in which they live. And at the same

time they are able to take part in the deadly serious power-in-action drama of political life. Very likely the violent can be co-opted into the political as readily as those of strong political persuasion are co-opted to violence.

Wolfgang and Ferracuti point to the need for breaking up and dispersing subcultures of violence, bodies of custom and value for the manifestation of violent behavior.[71] The nearer at hand and more visible is a body of custom for violence, the more will men turn to it when tension runs high. But there will be serious dangers in the attempt to fragment subcultures of violence. Subcultures are possessed by individuals. They are the social territories of those who make use of them.[72]

Any direct attempt to destroy these territorial possessions will lead to violent reaction by those who are committed to them. Negative ramifications will be less when oblique techniques are used. Thus the distraction of individuals from concern with subcultures of violence through the drawing power of innovation is a most useful if not inevitably necessary step. Once innovation has been experienced for some time, those who have held close allegiance to subcultures of violence can more readily take part in the destruction of those subcultures. Gradually they can bring to bear upon the breaking up of the bodies of violent custom those innovative techniques they have come to find rewarding.

The aforementioned co-optation of violent youth into the political realm, the formation by them of commitments to new programs for change, may lead to an interesting possibility. Those who once prized so highly the subcultures of violence can take arms against them with little danger of resistance. It is they themselves who would have thrown up the greatest defensive action. They can effectively burn their own bridges to violence behind them.

When innovation catches hold here and there, when severe competition abates slightly and when subcultures of violence lose some of their potency, it becomes less necessary for the young male defensively to "prove" himself a man. He can be less fearful of being a father beyond the stage of conception of a child simply because being a father will have become less difficult for him. His vision of himself as a unique person will slowly flower. His need to distort through gross magnification the unreciprocating machinations of others will grow less.

To achieve these changes, however, is a very great order indeed. However quietly it may be made to occur, nothing less than a fundamental shift in the way of life of a people is involved. For this reason alone, the chances of success will be poor. Yet the prospects of intentionally maintaining the *status quo* are even less.

9. *One Executioner**

Robert G. Elliott was chief executioner in New York State for many years. In his memoirs, *Agent of Death*, Elliott tells of his earlier interest in his chosen work. Later he explains his first steps in learning the role of executioner.[73]

"A crime occurred nine months later that was to result in the first inexplicable incident of my life. On March 6, 1894, in an election dispute at Troy, New York, a watcher at the polls was killed, and another shot, but not fatally. Bartholomew Shea was arrested for the murder; John B. McGough was charged with the other shooting. At their trials, the former was convicted of first-degree murder, and sentenced to die. The latter, also, was found guilty, receiving a long prison term.

"I was talking with George Tozier, son of a Brockport druggist, when the papers reached us with the news that Shea was to be electrocuted. Strangely enough, my thoughts turned from the doomed man to the one who by the mere closing of an electric switch, would quickly dispatch Shea into the next world.

" 'Think of the executioner's great responsibility,' " I declared. 'That's a job I'd like to have.'

"An expression of horror spread over Tozier's face. He looked at me unbelievingly, as though he had not heard correctly. Then the full significance of what I had said dawned on me. I hurriedly changed the subject, and I guess he did not take my statement seriously. Surely neither of us ever dreamed that the day would come when I was to be engaged in such work.

"What impelled that remark, I do not know. Often I have

*From the book, *Agent of Death: The Memoirs of an Executioner* by Robert G. Elliott and Albert Beatty. Copyright, 1940 by Albert R. Beatty. Published by E. P. Dutton & Co., Inc. and used with their permission.

tried to explain it to myself, but without success. Perhaps I entertained the opinion that a high degree of science was required to kill human beings painlessly; that the man who served as executioner must be a clever electrician."

Years later, Elliott served as prison electrician. Three men were to be hanged. Davis, a migrant executioner, had not arrived. The warden asked Elliott to perform the executions if Davis failed to appear.

" 'There's really nothing to it,' declared the warden. 'With what you know about electricity, you wouldn't have any trouble at all. One of the guards who attends every execution could show you anything you didn't quite understand. Of course, if it's a case of not wanting to do the job, that's a different matter.'

"Both of us remained silent for several minutes. The warden was the first to speak.

" 'Suppose the Van Wormers had killed your father. Wouldn't you be willing to throw the switch on them then? Frankly, I don't relish this thing any more than you do. It's a nasty business, this taking men out and killing them. But it has to be done, and I suppose they've got it coming to them.'

"Warden Deyo rose from his chair, and started pacing up and down again.

" 'Those executions tomorrow have me worried,' he confided. 'The whole world is watching this case, and the slightest mishap will bring all kinds of criticism down on our heads. I wish the governor would do something, but I don't think he will. His wife has been begging him for the last few days to save the boys. I imagine he's more uneasy than I am.'

"At this point, Davis walked into the room. I do not know when I was ever so glad to see anybody. Warden Deyo told him of our fears, and the executioner appeared much amused. Davis explained that the reason for his arrival at this hour was that he had taken a later train than usual, and it was delayed en route.

"Walking home that night, I pondered whether I would have taken Davis' place at the controls had he failed to report in time for the executions. I came to the conclusion that I would have. I was, after all, in the prison service, and considered it my duty to comply with the warden's requests.

"The next day dawned with threatening skies. When I arrived at the prison, I learned that the three youths had passed a sleepless night, tossing uneasily on their cots. It was the decision of Burton and Fred that Willis, the oldest but most nervous and distraught of the boys, should go to the chair first. Fred, the youngest, was to follow; then Burton, who it was believed could best endure those last terrifying minutes about which you and I can know little.

"At 11:15 a.m., the bell sounded to start the engine. Thirty-five minutes later came the signal to cut off the current. Three men had paid with their lives for the one they had taken. I stopped the generator, changed the armature, and left the prison to return home for lunch.

"My house was but two blocks from the prison, so it did not take me long to reach it. As I opened the front door, the bell of the old-fashioned wall telephone was ringing. My wife answered the call.

"'It's for you,' she said, handing me the receiver. 'Whoever it is, is awfully excited about something.'

"The call was from Billy Roberts, a trusty assigned to duty in the power plant and about whom I will have more to say later.

"'Come back!' he shouted. 'Davis says to hurry! There's trouble!'

"I dashed out of the house without a word to my wife, and was at the prison plant in less than three minutes. Davis was waiting for me.

"'Get the engine going,' he ordered. 'One of the boys is alive. We've got to put him back in the chair.' The executioner hastened to the death chamber.

"Feverishly, I brought the power up to the required voltage. The signal came to turn on the current. A few minutes later, Davis appeared at the plant.

"'Stop the engine,' he said. 'We won't need the current. He died before we got him in the chair.'

"I shut off the power, and went up to the death chamber. There I learned what had happened. The 1,700 volts which had coursed through the straining body of Fred Van Wormer, the youngest of the three murderers, had not killed him. Taken from the chair after the doctors had pronounced him dead, his body had been laid in an adjoining room to await the customary autopsy. A guard, Will Parsons, chanced in the room after the executions were over, and saw Fred's hand move and an eye flicker. He ran out of the room calling for the prison physician, who had already started to examine Willis and Burton.

" 'He moved!' Parsons yelled, pointing in the direction of the slab on which Fred lay. 'I saw him move! We've got to do something quick!'

"An immediate investigation proved that the guard was right. Fred's heart, larger than that of any other person electrocuted up to that time, was still beating, and he was alive. There was only one thing to do: put him in the chair again, and pass current through his body until he was dead.

"It was a very much puzzled Davis who talked with me later about the incident. 'I can't understand it,' he said. 'I gave him two shocks of the full current, and kept it on two minutes. The doctors were so sure he was dead I didn't bother with a third one. I wish now I had.'

"Not a word about Fred Van Wormer's brief survival reached outside the prison. Newspapers informed their readers that the three brothers went to the chair 'without one unforeseen incident to mar the perfect and dignified execution of the death penalty imposed by the trial court.' Several did, however, mention the fact that when a group of some fifty long-termers saw the witnesses leaving the death house, they displayed their resentment at what had happened by hissing and uttering hideous shrieks. Demonstrations of this sort among convicts on execution days were not uncommon, and at times were difficult to check.

"Superintendent Collins met me shortly afterward, and asked if I had witnessed the triple execution. I replied that I had not, and explained the reason. He instructed me to accompany Davis to Sing Sing when the next execution was scheduled there. At this one, he told me, I was merely to observe how the state kills a man; at subsequent ones, I was to help Davis. But nothing was said about my ever being called upon to throw the switch. As one of Davis' assistants, I was to receive additional compensation. I accepted the assignment."

At a later point Elliott took over Davis' position as executioner.

PART II:

INWARD DIRECTED,
PERSONAL VIOLENCE:
SUICIDE

CHAPTER V

Theory and Suicide

1. *Durkheim and Social Integration*

It is not usual to consider suicide as a form of violence.[1] Yet suicide quite obviously is as violent as homicide by any reasonable standard. Much in agreement with Durkheim,[2] suicide is defined here as the killing of oneself other than accidentally. At basis, suicide is a rage against society directed toward the self. It will be clear that suicide and homicide are highly similar and highly dissimilar. The purposeful taking of human life is the most apparent similarity, yet the distinction between killing another and oneself is obviously very great. As has been discussed many times, suicide may contain a large component of outward directed agression: the suicidal person may through his self-destruction bring about guilt and remorse in those with whom he has interacted closely.[3] And criminal homicide may involve a significant degree of inward directed aggression: by his violent act the offender may in part be attempting to bring punishment—life imprisonment or death—upon himself.

The sociological analysis of suicide has produced a considerable body of literature in which researchers have built solidly on the work of those who came before them.[4] Durkheim's influence has of course extended far beyond the analysis of suicide *per se*. He was a founding father of the equilibrium school of social thought.[5] His view that crime and deviance in general enhanced social solidarity has had an extraordinarily widespread impact on sociological theory.[6] It is the starting point for most sociological approaches that hold deviance to have positive social uses or at least not necessarily to have negative consequences for a society.[7]

Several writers have discussed Durkheim's conservatism, his concern for the normal, and his aversion to conflict.[8] That aver-

93

sion he may have had and his equation of the unusual in social life with the pathological is clear. Nevertheless, his view of criminal deviance takes into account a considerable degree of conflict and violence between the non-criminal majority and the criminal minority.'[9] On the one hand the two conspire, as it were, in the perpetuation of the social organization. But they are in conflict as they do so: Criminals lash out at the majority and the majority retaliates with legitimized punishment. For Durkheim, crimes are acts that always "evoke from society the particular reaction called punishment. . . . We call every punished act a crime."[10]

In his analysis of suicide Durkheim placed great stress on social integration, yet the meaning he assigned to the term has never been completely clear to others.[11] As suggested in the beginning chapter, he seems to have meant the degree to which a society or group is characterized by agreement about basic life values.[12] Durkheim saw egoistic suicide as due to a widespread, perpetual absence of social integration. Anomic suicide was a consequence of sudden decreases in individuals' integration into society. Hence the anomic form is actually a variant of the egoistic. Durkheim held further that social integration and altruistic suicide are positively related. That is, as integration grows excessive, the extent of the institutionalization of suicide for "the good of the society" increases. Durkheim believed, then, that the extremes of both high and low social integration gave rise to suicide.[13]

One can with some reason take the view that the more do people agree about fundamental values, the more will they cooperate and reciprocate with one another.[14] Thus, seen in this way, Durkheim's formulation would suggest that suicide is generated by high levels of reciprocity and of unreciprocity in social life and by severe drops in reciprocity as well.[15]

2. *Four Contemporary Theories of Suicide*

Gibbs and Martin, using Durkheim's work as a departure point, set forth a status integration theory of suicide.[16] Their central idea is that: The more usual is it in a population for individuals to hold given sets of statuses—that is, the more are statuses commonly associated with one another—the greater is status integration. And their major theorem holds that a population's suicide rate varies inversely with status integration. The Gibbs and Martin conceptualization is essentially one of role conflict cast in status terms. As those authors say, an individual is confronted with incompatibility of statuses when conforming to the role of one status interferes with conforming to the roles of others.[17]

A basic problem in the Gibbs and Martin formulation is that the degree to which statuses are commonly associated with one another is not necessarily an inverse measure of role conflict. By example most physicians in the United States are married. Yet there seem no grounds for assuming that married physicians experience less role conflict than unmarried physicians. In fact it may well be that the juxtaposition of the married and medical roles generate much conflict.[18] On the other hand a major asset of the status integration formulation is its amenability to empirical test.

In any case, status integration implies reciprocity in role relationships. According to Gibbs and Martin, the more do performances for given individuals interfere with one another, the lower is status integration. From the perspective set forth in chapter one, unreciprocity in interaction is a primary source of interference among role performances. Thus if unreciprocity and reciprocity are substituted for status integration in the Gibbs and Martin theory, the following would be predicted: Suicide will increase as reciprocity decreases and unreciprocity increases.

Like Durkheim, Powell writes of both excessive social integration and disintegration as giving rise to suicide.[19] Two opposite types of anomie result from these extremes, Powell suggests. One is a consequence of the individual's dissociation from the culture, the other of his envelopment by it. "Both render the individual impotent and thus both give rise to self-contempt which in extreme cases eventuates in suicide."[20] Again, envelopment by the culture might be construed to imply excessive reciprocity in role relationships and dissociation from the culture to imply extreme unreciprocity. Extremes of either—reciprocity or unreciprocity—would then be seen as forces behind suicide.

③ Straus and Straus take the position that the more a society is closely structured—the more are reciprocal duties stressed and enforced and the less is variation in individual behavior positively sanctioned—the higher will be the incidence of suicide; and as noted earlier the lower the incidence of criminal homicide.[21] Straus and Straus are explicit in the view that in a closely structured society, homicide is not a culturally permissible solution to conflict whereas suicide is. Here is a straightforward statement of a hypothesis that in the general sense accords with the formulation set forth in the present analysis: Suicide increases as reciprocity in role relationships grows greater. The reasoning behind that hypothesis will be reviewed shortly.

④ Henry and Short argue that suicide is characteristic of high prestige groups and homicide of low prestige groups.[22] They hold that as prestige increases, there is a decrease in the strength of the relational system, that is, in the extent to which individuals are involved in social or cathectic relationships with others. Further they take the position that as prestige increases, there is a decrease in the strength of external restraint—the degree to which behavior is required to conform to the demands and expectations of others.[23] In sum, this is Henry and Short's position: As prestige of individuals becomes greater and external restraints and the strength of the relational system grow less suicide increases; and as prestige becomes lower and restraints and strength of the relational system grow greater, homicide increases. Those authors write: "When behavior is subjected to strong external restraint by virtue either of subordinate status or intense involvement in social relationships with other persons, it is easy to blame others when frustration occurs. But when the restraints are weak, the self must bear the responsibility for frustration."[24] Strong external restraints mean conflict among individuals while weak restraints imply an absence of conflict.[25]

Everything considered, external restraints indicate unreciprocity in role relationships.[26] Hence in a reconstruction of the Henry and Short approach, one should find that unreciprocity generates homicide and reciprocity suicide. The matter is complicated, however, by the fact that strong relational systems do not necessarily imply unreciprocity; they may mean high reciprocity. Yet for Henry and Short, strong relational systems are associated with strong external restraints.

3. *Social Disorganization, Downward Mobility, and Loss*

Halwachs was among the first to stress a connection between urbanization and suicide.[27] His was essentially a subcultural formulation. He saw the urban subculture as one of particularly great conflict in patterned social relations.[28] Roughly speaking, in the Halwachs formulation, conflict in social relations means unreciprocity which in turn leads to suicide.

Cavan,[29] Schmid,[30] and others[31] have pursued with tenacity and ingenuity the possibilities of relationships between the lower-class core areas of cities and suicide. Viewing those areas as highly disorganized, Cavan finds that they give rise to high suicide rates.[32] For Cavan, it is disorder and instability that spell suicide; order and stability do not. Schmid's results are essentially similar.[33] Faris sums up the case for the "social disorganization school": "Suicide therefore usually reflects a failure of social control over the behavior of the person, and . . . is connected with various indications of individualism and detachment. It is therefore, in our society, clearly a phenomenon of social disorganization."[34]

However, relatively recent research and reinterpretation of earlier research have indicated the following: What were traditionally viewed as disorganized areas of the city are in fact often quite highly organized.[35] As but one illustration, one that will be elaborated shortly, skid row areas are characterized by much smoothly functioning, patterned interaction despite the high rate of turnover of the population.[36] So to some degree are various types of tenement areas, ghetto and otherwise, in large cities.[37] Reciprocity is far from absent in so-called disorganized areas. In some cases it may have been the researchers' ethnocentric, moralistic attitude that led them to characterize as disorganized areas with high rates of suicide and of other forms of deviance.[38]

A closely related matter is the consistent finding that downwardly mobile individuals congregate in "disorganized" areas. And those individuals are especially prone to suicide.[39] A number of reports indicate a positive relation between loss of status (prestige) and suicide.[40] Breed and others have found a distinct tendency for downward occupational mobility to be associated with suicide.[41] Further data regarding downward mobility as it may generate suicide are presented in the following chapter.[42]

Wood points to the threat of downward mobility as a crucial variable. Stressing the need to combine the individual's subjectively felt condition with observations of the objectively observed social system, Wood finds suicide to be largely a high status phenomenon. Speaking of Ceylon he writes: "Not high status *per se*, but relatively high status in conjunction with stress from an insecure achieved position is the structural component of a high suicide rate."[43]

Other researchers have widened the idea of downward social mobility and conceived of various types of social loss as major variables behind suicide. Psychologist George Kelly's personal construct theory is of special relevance here. It is Kelly's view that "a person's processes are psychologically channeled by the ways in which he anticipates events."[44] That is, how he construes the future determines what he does in the present. Personal constructs are channels for anticipating events, they are guides to the future.[45]

Regarding role, Kelly writes: "Let us suppose that one person attempts to understand another, not merely as a behaving object or merely in terms of stimulus input and response output, but as another person who himself has an outlook tingeing all of his perceptions of the world about him. If, seeing the other person in this manner, a person goes on to regulate his own behavior in reference to such a subsuming construction, then he is enacting a social *role*."[46] Kelly takes the position that when an individual construes himself as having lost one or more roles that he once possessed, then guilt ensues and the likelihood of suicide increases.

Gibbs's earlier work on suicide centered on the previously noted idea of status integration. More recently he has postulated "*disruption of social relations* as *the* etiological factor in suicide."[47] Gibbs states two propositions: "(1) The greater the incidence of disrupted social relations in a population, the higher the suicide rate of that population; and (2) All suicide victims have experienced a set of disrupted social relations that is not found in the history of non-victims."[48] Gibbs refers to a wide range of disruptions, of instances where patterns of social relation between persons are interrupted. He speaks of "the death of a parent, spouse, or child; separation; divorce; termination of employment; some types of residential changes; the termination of a love affair; and some changes in employment situations, to mention only a few possibilities."[49]

4. *Common Threads*

When the various theoretical formulations of suicide set forth above are surveyed, the themes of reciprocity, unreciprocity and social integration stand out as they did in relation to homicide. Gibbs and Martin refer, although in other terms, to unreciprocity in social relations as a major force behind suicide. Straus and Straus speak explicitly and Henry and Short implicitly of high reciprocity as generator of suicide. Durkheim and Powell view suicide as a consequence of two extremes in social life, extremes similar to widespread reciprocity and unreciprocity in status-role relations. Breed, Kelly and, recently, Gibbs place major emphasis on the loss of roles as a paramount condition giving rise to suicide.[50]

As was discussed at the outset, reciprocity and low tension in role relations imply social integration. Unreciprocity and high tension indicate a lack of social integration. Generally, sociological and social psychological theories have stressed that suicide is a consequence of extremely high or low levels of social integration or of both. Theories of homicide tend to emphasize low social integration, or variants of it, as the major source of outward directed violence.

To put the matter in everyday terms, theoretical approaches to suicide and homicide cannot have it both ways. While distinctly different forms of suicide might be explained by opposite extremes of integration, the same forms cannot legitimately be so explained. Some approaches predict that one extreme of integration will generate suicide in general while others predict that the opposite will lead to one or more particular forms of suicide. As an example, Straus and Straus predict that close structuring of society has as a consequence high suicide rates while Durkheim predicts that excessive social integration means much altruistic suicide.

Further, some theoretical formulations predict that homicide will result from low levels of social integration and others predict that suicide will arise because of similar levels of integration. Again, to illustrate: Straus and Straus suggest that loose structuring of a society means high homicide rates while Gibbs and Martin argue that low status integration leads to high suicide rates.

Beginning at this juncture and continuing through the next two chapters, it will be the central aim to show that from the standpoint of social systems suicide is generated by either of the following: sustained low tension (and excessively high reciprocity); or by large-scale drops in tension (and increases in reciprocity) of those systems. In a parallel sense, suicidal behavior by given individuals is seen as brought about by continuing low tension or by severe decreases in tension of their inner systems.

There need not be loss of roles for a state of low tension to exist in either a social or inner system. There may simply obtain over a long period a series of small processes that bring about a condition of high reciprocity among roles in a social system; or in the case of the inner system, that lead to little self-perceived interference among the individual's performances. Those processes are discussed later.

On the other hand, low tension in a social system is often due in large measure to the widespread loss, dropping out, of roles. Since there are fewer roles to generate unreciprocity, reciprocity or at least an absence of unreciprocity obtains by default, as it were. (Illustrative here was the massive unemployment of the early 1930's in this country.) Similarly, low tension in the inner system of the individual can be a consequence of his loss of roles.

Having a smaller number of roles to play, he is likely to perceive less interference among his performances.[51]

5. *Low Tension in Social Systems*

The idea of low tension in social systems as a possible source of deviance and of self-directed violence in particular is little understood. And in fact in a society such as that of the United States, the concept of low tension in the social environment is poorly comprehended regardless of any relationship to violence. (The literature concerning the idea of low tension is very sparse indeed.[52]) This is in part due to the fact that we are as a people extremely fearful of low tension in the environment.[53] Thus it will be useful to devote the remainder of this chapter to some illustrations of situations and social systems in low tension and to various reactions to these phenomena.

An apt example of a group which in the main experiences social systems in extremely low tension is the Hutterites.[54] Eaton and Weil describe their daily life: It "provides social security from the womb to the tomb. It promised absolute salvation to all who follow its precepts."[55] "'Do the best you can' rather than a competitive slogan, is characteristic of the entire life cycle."[56] They are "extreme in their emphasis on social cohesiveness."[57] As Eaton and Weil go on to say, "The strong social cohesion and clear-cut expectations which tend to protect Hutterites from having to face the uncertainties of life unaided and without normative guidance, can also be a source of psychological stress."[58] Rates for depressive mental disorders are in fact extremely high among the Hutterites.

Skid Road areas frequently display high reciprocity and low tension despite discussions of them as disorganized.[59] As Jackson and Connor report: "There is a common definition among alcoholics that Skid Road is a refuge...."[60] The group provides "unqualified acceptance" for members, those authors state. "When the alcoholic who has been off Skid Road for a time returns he feels a relaxation of tension and a sense of leaving his worries behind him."[61] Suicide rates in various skid road areas have in a number of studies been found to be high.[62] Alcoholism can in itself be construed as a form of self-directed aggression.[63]

Huxley's *Brave New World* is a fictional account which exemplifies excessive reciprocity, low tension, in the social system. With few exceptions, there is a place for everyone and everyone is in his place. Reciprocity is the order of the day. All proceeds with machine-like precision. And that is the dehumanizing trouble with the "brave new world."

The Hopi possess a highly reciprocating way of life.[64] The individual makes room for the other person, defers to him. He helps another to win rather than attempting to win himself. The Hopi exhibit little outward-directed aggression. On the other hand, the extreme form of self-directed aggression, suicide, is exceedingly prevalent.[65] In partial contrast traditional Maori life was characterized by widescale shifts in levels of tension. Broadly speaking, low reciprocity in role relationships and hence low tensions were usual throughout the society for a period of perhaps a year; these were replaced by high reciprocity and low tension for a similar period; then the cycle was repeated[66] Both murder and suicide rates were extremely high among the Maori.[67] Murder appears to have been especially prevalent toward the end of the high tension phase of the cycle and suicide toward the end of the low tension phase.[68]

The robot-like, hand-in-glove routine of situations of much reciprocity and little tension is exceedingly stultifying to participants. The lack of challenge, the absence of social friction, provides a weightlessness in social space that is as frustrating and as terrifying as low reciprocity and high tension. Yet participants recognize that all is proceeding "as it should," in organized fashion, according to plan. However, if excessive frustration is experienced, the individual is likely to feel that someone must bear the responsibility. Others cannot be blamed: they do not block performances; on the contrary, they facilitate them. The individual turns to himself. He sees himself as responsible for the pain he feels under "ideal" environmental conditions. He retreats, the self is blamed, and aggression is directed inward.[69]

Abrupt and large-scale decreases in the tension levels of social systems pose especially great problems for those individuals who participate in them. At an earlier time there has been either the rewarding innovation of moderate tension or the frustrating strain of eyeball-to-eyeball high tension. Suddenly there is the shock of rapid decompression. Tension that has supported the social system, that has given it its form, is to a considerable degree no longer there. If participants have lost roles in this process, they are unlikely to blame others. For it is not others who tend to be perceived as responsible. Consider an elderly upper-middle-class widower. The youngest child has grown, married, left home; that is what children are supposed to do. The man's job as vice-president of a small company is gone because of mandatory retirement. He has lost his wife because of a terminal illness. Thus the pensioned widower sits affluently in the sun and silence and dies either slowly or, by his own hand, quickly.

We in the United States are relatively unused to social environments in low tension. We talk as though they were highly desirable and we do our utmost to avoid them. Social systems in low tension are what so many devoutly wish for and cannot in fact abide. Living so much of the time, as we do, in high tension social systems composed of confrontational situations, the opposite is popularly construed as a promised land. The peacefulness of full reciprocity is yearned for and feared. The highly prized weightlessness in social space turns out to be unending sameness, a void, that spells stagnation and decay.[70] There is on the part of many an intuitive feeling that such an environment is harmful. Thus individuals are ingenious at creating only the form rather than the substance of low tension social systems.

However, if that ingenuity fails and an overly placid environment obtains, then men blame themselves for the severe frustration they feel. They aggress against themselves. In the ultimate, they kill themselves.

CHAPTER VI

Suicide and the Social System

1. *Suicide Rates Around the World*

As with homicide, suicide rates for societies around the world vary substantially. Broadly speaking, rates for suicide are four to five times as high as homicide rates. Table 7 gives rates for 41 literate societies, *circa* 1962: The median rate (per 100,000 population) is approximately 8.0. While the United States ranks high relative to other countries in regard to homicide, this is somewhat less the case for suicide. With a rate of 10.8, the United States ranks sixteenth among the 41 countries.

It will be useful to compare the five countries having the highest annual rates with the five having the lowest. In the highest group are Hungary, 24.9; Austria, 22.4; Finland, 22.1; Czechoslovakia, 20.6; and West Germany, 18.7. Those that comprise the lowest group are: United Arab Republic, 0.1; Jordan, 0.2; Nicaragua, 0.4; Dominican Republic, 1.0; and Peru, 1.4. Countries in the high group are European and well industrialized. Those in the low group are Latin American and Middle Eastern and tend to be in the throes of moving from technologically unadvanced to advanced status. All in all it might be said that the low-rate countries are experiencing great culture change, and the high-rate much less change.

An analysis of 40 non-literate societies shows wide variation also.[1] Societies were rated on a 22-point scale where zero indicated absence of suicide; a rating of 11 was equivalent to a rate of 9.0 in literate societies and 21 to a rate of 25.0.[2] Ratings varied from 21 to zero. The median rating was between five and six which, comparatively, is somewhat below the median of 8.0 for literate societies.

The 40 societies were rated also as to the overall degree of reciprocity in role relationships in everyday life.[3] Table 8 indi-

TABLE 7—*Suicide Rates for 41 Countries,* circa 1962

Country	Rate per 100,000	Year	Country	Rate per 100,000	Year
Hungary	24.9	1962	New Zealand	8.4	1962
Austria	22.4	1962	Bulgaria	8.0	1962
Finland	22.1	1962	Chile	7.7	1961
Czechoslovakia	20.6	1961	Netherlands	6.6	1962
Germany, West	18.7	1961	Norway	6.6	1961
Switzerland	18.2	1961	Panama	6.4	1962
Japan	17.3	1962	Italy	5.6	1961
Denmark	16.9	1961	Spain	5.5	1960
Sweden	16.9	1961	Colombia	4.8	1962
France	15.1	1962	Greece	3.4	1962
Belgium	14.7	1961	Guatemala	3.1	1962
Union of			Costa Rica	2.4	1962
South Africa	14.2[a]	1960	Mexico	1.9	1960
Australia	13.7	1962	Ireland	1.8	1962
United Kingdom	11.6[c]	1962	Peru	1.4	1959
Uruguay	11.3	1955	Dominican		
United States	10.8	1962	Republic	1.0	1960
Ceylon	9.9	1960	Nicaragua	0.4	1962
Iceland	9.4	1962	Jordan	0.2	1962
Luxembourg	9.3	1962	United Arab		
Poland	8.8	1961	Republic	0.1[b]	1961
Portugal	8.6	1962			

Source: *Demographic Yearbook, 1963* (New York: United Nations, 1964), Table 25.

[a] White population only.

[b] Population within Health Bureau localities only.

[c] Rate based on 1961 population.

From: Jack P. Gibbs, "Suicide," in Robert K. Merton and Robert A. Nisbet, *Contemporary Social Problems* (New York: Harcourt, Brace and World, 1966) p. 297.

cates that of the 20 societies above the median for suicide, 13 were above the median for reciprocity and but seven were below it. Of the 20 societies below the suicide median, 13 were also below the reciprocity median and the remaining seven were above it. Here, then, is evidence in favor of the hypothesis that as reciprocity in societies grows great and tension low, the incidence of suicide increases. Data given in an earlier chapter regarding the relationship between homicide and reciprocity are repeated in Table 8. The comparison between suicide and homicide is striking. There is a strong positive relationship between suicide

TABLE 8—*Numbers of Non-Literate Societies Above and Below Median*
Scores for Reciprocity in Role Relationships
and for Suicide and Homicide

| | SUICIDE | | | HOMICIDE | | |
	Below Median	Above Median	Total	Below Median	Above Median	Total
High Reciprocity (Above Median)	7	13	20	14	6	20
Low Reciprocity* (Below Median)	13	7	20	7	13	20
Total	20	20	40	21	19	40

*Includes unreciprocity.

and reciprocity and a strong inverse relationship between homicide and reciprocity.

2. *The Relation Between Suicide and Homicide Rates*

At the same time, an interesting finding of the non-literate
study is the rather close positive relationship between suicide and
homicide ratings. Those societies that have a high incidence of
suicide tend also to have a high incidence of homicide; those low
on suicide tend to be low on homicide. Table 9 indicates that 13
of the 20 societies above the mean rating for suicide are also
above the mean rating for homicide. And 14 of the 20 societies
below the median rating for suicide are below the median homicide rating.[4]

The aforementioned traditional Maori exemplify the societies
with high ratings of both suicide and homicide.[5] The yearly alter-
nation in Maori life between one extreme of cooperative reciprocity and the other extreme of competitive unreciprocity seems
to have given rise respectively to suicide and homicide. The peak
period of reciprocity was followed by a suicidal wave and the
peak of unreciprocity by an excess of homicide.[6] The contemporary Lapp, on the other hand, are aptly illustrative of non-literate
societies with very low rates of both suicide and homicide. Lapp
social life is not characterized by extremes of reciprocity or
unreciprocity. It exemplifies, rather, moderate degrees of both.[7]
Getting a living is hard for the Lapps. They are challenged by

TABLE 9—*Non-Literate Societies Above and Below the Median Ratings for Suicide and Homicide**

	BELOW SUICIDE MEDIAN		ABOVE SUICIDE MEDIAN	
Above Homicide Median	18—Yungar	—0	21—Jivaro	— 8
	11—Rwala	—2	21—Maori	—21
	9—Alorese	—1	18—Muria	—18
	9—Samoans	—5	15—Ashanti	—18
	9—Thonga	—2	15—Chukchee	—15
	9—Kaska	—2	15—Trukese	—12
			14—Ainu	—12
			14—Azande	— 6
			14—Chagga	—11
			12—Copper Eskimo	— 6
			12—Lamba	—12
			12—Tiv	— 9
			11—Comanche	—21
Below Homicide Median	8—Omaha	—2	8—Bena	—14
	6—Lovedu	—4	6—Kwakiutl	— 6
	6—Papago	—2	6—Navaho	— 8
	6—Sanpoil	—5	5—Marquesans	— 8
	5—Aymara	—4	3—Hopi	—18
	3—Ifugao	—2	3—Taos	— 6
	3—Trobrianders	—5	2—Lepcha	—12
	3—Zuni	—0		
	2—Andamans	—0		
	2—Ifaluk	—2		
	1—Wogeo	—2		
	0—Lapp	—0		
	0—Tanala	—3		
	0—Tikopia	—3		

*The number that precedes a society's name indicates that society's rating for homicide. The number that immediately follows a society's name indicates the rating for suicide. Adapted from: Stuart Palmer, "Murder and Suicide in Forty Non-Literate Societies," *Journal of Criminal Law, Criminology and Police Science*, Vol. 56 (Sept., 1965), pp. 320-24.

their environment but not overwhelmingly so. They must cooperate to some considerable degree if they are to survive; and yet they place much stress on independence. The Lapp are an extremely dynamic people on the one hand and they possess an extraordinarily non-violent social life on the other.

The positive association between suicide and homicide is not generally found among literate societies. For those societies, an inverse relation between the two forms of violence is usual.[8]

Wood presents data for 36 literate societies for various years between 1951 and 1956. (See Table 10.) The 13 countries classified by Wood as possessing a high homicide rate have a median suicide rate of 4.5. That is considerably below the median suicide rate of 8.5 for all 36 countries. The 13 countries classified by Wood as having low homicide rates show a median suicide rate of 10.7. However, the 10 countries in the moderate homicide category have an even higher median suicide rate of 17.9. If one divides the 36 countries into quartiles by homicide and suicide rates, as in Table 11, the tendency for homicide and suicide rates to vary inversely with each other is shown in somewhat sharper focus.

Two of many studies that indicate inverse relationships between suicide and homicide are those by Henry and Short and by Porterfield et al. Regarding their detailed study of connections between suicide and homicide and changes in the business cycle, Henry and Short say: "Our data show that while suicide rises in depression and falls in prosperity, crimes of violence against persons rise in prosperity and fall during depression. Although suicide of all categories increases during depression, the degree of increase is greatest among the high status (prestige) categories ... (which) suffer a greater relative loss of statuses during business contraction than do low status categories.... As we move down the status scale, the response of suicide to business depression decreases and the response of homicide to business prosperity increases."[9] The Henry and Short results, then, support the conviction that social loss is a generating force behind suicide. Less directly those results support also the idea that blockage to social goals plays a part in the homicidal process: the lower the prestige of individuals, the more is it possible for their goals to be denied and the more in fact are they denied.

Porterfield and his colleagues explored the relationship between "social well-being" of states in this country and suicide.[10] (Social well-being was based on a variety of measures of economic welfare, education, and "culture" living conditions, medical facilities, and health.) Indices of social well-being and of rates of suicide for the various states yielded a coefficient of correlation of .82. Social well-being clearly reflects a life style

Suicide and the Social System

TABLE 10—Suicide and Homicide Rates for 36 Literate Societies, 1951-1956* (Rates per 100,000 population)ᵃ

High Homicide Rateᵇ		Moderate Homicide Rateᵇ		Low Homicide Rateᵇ	
Country	Suicide Rate	Country	Suicide Rate	Country	Suicide Rate
Egypt (3.5)	.3	Poland (1.2)	5.6	Ireland (.4)	2.3
Mexico (39.1)	1.1	Italy (1.9)	6.5	North Ireland (.5)	3.4
Colombia (32.7)	1.3	Portugal (1.4)	9.7	Spain (1.1)	5.9
Taiwan (23.0)	2.0	Australia (1.5)	10.4	Scotland (.7)	6.0
Costa Rica (4.1)	2.8	Singapore (1.9)	11.4	Netherlands (.6)	6.2
Guatemala (6.7)	2.8	Finland (3.1)	17.9	Canada (1.1)	7.2
Dominican Rep. (4.9)	3.5	Hungary (2.1)	19.3	Norway (.4)	7.2
Chile (9.1)	4.5	Japan (2.2)	21.2	England, Wales (.7)	10.7
Ceylon (4.3)	7.3	Switzerland (1.2)	2.17	Belgium (.8)	13.5
U.S.A. (4.8)	10.1	Austria (1.2)	23.1	France (.7)	15.6
Hawaii (4.1)	10.5			Sweden (.7)	17.5
Uruguay (4.7)	11.2			West Germany (1.0)	18.6
Puerto Rico (7.3)	12.4			Denmark (.9)	23.4

Median rates for 36 countries: homicide, 1.7; suicide, 8.5.

Source: Compiled from United Nations, *Demographic Yearbook*, 3-9 issues, New York, 1951-1957.

ᵃRates are based on average rates for two to five years as available between 1951 and 1956, eliminating years with gross internal disturbances, i.e., Hungary, 1956, and war conditions.

ᵇAverage homicide rates appear within parentheses. Those countries within the middle 25th percentile range of the array of average homicide rates are classed as having a "moderate" homicide rate; "high" and "low" categories include countries on either side of this range, respectively. Countries are ranked by suicide average rates within each homicide category.

*Arthur Lewis Wood, "Crime and Aggression in Changing Ceylon", *Transactions of the American Philosophical Society* (December, 1961), New Series Volume 51, part 8, p. 55.

TABLE 11—*Suicide versus Homicide Rates in 36 Literate Societies*

Homicide Rate in:	Suicide Rate in:			
	Highest Quartile	Second Quartile	Third Quartile	Lowest Quartile
Highest Quartile	N=0	N=3 United States Uruguay Puerto Rico	N=1 Chile	N=5 Mexico Colombia Taiwan Guatemala Dominican Rep.
Second Quartile	N=3 Finland Hungary Japan	N=2 Hawaii Singapore	N=2 Ceylon Italy	N=2 Egypt Costa Rica
Third Quartile	N=4 Switzerland Austria West Germany Denmark	N=2 Portugal Australia	N=3 Poland Spain Canada	N=0
Lowest Quartile	N=2 France Sweden	N=2 England, Wales Belgium	N=3 Scotland Netherlands Norway	N=2 Ireland North Ireland

Adapted from: Arthur Lewis Wood, "Crime and Aggression in Changing Ceylon," *Transactions of the American Philosophical Society* (December, 1961), New Series Volume 51, part 8, p. 55.

that emphasizes helping others, reciprocity in role relationships. Here in the positive association between social well-being and suicide rates is tangible evidence that high reciprocity (low tension in the social system) gives rise to suicide.

3. Geography and Migration

There is a tendency for suicide rates to be low in most northern regions of the United States and high in the west. (See Table 12.) It is worth noting that the non-white rate is lowest in the south while the white rate is lowest in the north. Suicide rates are especially high in the upper reaches of New England and are quite low in the Deep South.[11] In contrast, homicide rates are very low in northern New England and high in the Deep South.

As noted in chapter two, reciprocity in everyday life is high in northern New England. In the Deep South, the enormous problems of race relations insure a high degree of unreciprocity.

TABLE 12—*Suicide Rates for Regions of the United States by Sex and Color, 1960*

Region*	WHITE			NON-WHITE		
	Male	*Female*	*Total*	*Male*	*Female*	*Total*
North	16.0	5.0	10.4	7.4	2.2	4.7
South	18.5	4.5	11.4	6.0	1.4	3.6
West	22.0	8.4	15.2	12.7	4.9	8.9
U.S.	17.6	5.4	11.4	7.1	1.9	4.4

*Regions: *North*: Maine, New Hampshire, Vermont, Massachusetts, Rhode Island, Connecticut, New York, New Jersey, Pennsylvania, Ohio, Indiana, Illinois, Michigan, Wisconsin, Minnesota, Iowa, Missouri, North Dakota, South Dakota, Nebraska, and Kansas; *South*: Delaware, Maryland, District of Columbia, Virginia, West Virginia, North Carolina, South Carolina, Georgia, Florida, Kentucky, Tennessee, Alabama, Mississippi, Arkansas, Louisiana, Oklahoma, and Texas; *West*: Montana, Idaho, Wyoming, Colorado, New Mexico, Arizona, Utah, Nevada, Washington, Oregon, and California.

Source: *Vital Statistics of the United States, 1960*, Vol. II, Mortality, Office of Vital Statistics (Washington, D.C.), pp. 125-379. *United States Census of Population, 1960: United States Summary, General Population Characteristics*, Bureau of the Census (Washington, D.C.), pp. 159, 160, and 167-72.

From Sanford Labovitz, "Variation in Suicide Rates," in Jack P. Gibbs, *Suicide* (New York: Harper and Row, 1968), p. 62.

Again regarding the upper reaches of New England, there is an abiding sense of loss. Farming simply cannot be carried on effectively by traditional methods. Yet it is those methods that are considered by the native to be the only effective ones.[12] He farms by the old ways and he fails. The self is blamed. In contrast, the southern black does not for the most part experience loss at the hands of southern whites for he has so little to lose. He does experience a sense of blockage and he blames those whites.

Historically, it has been usual for the urban suicide rate to exceed the rural rate in most countries around the world.[13] During recent decades, however, there has been a tendency for the gap between urban and rural rates to lessen. Table 13 shows that there were in 1960 but very small differences in rates for urban and rural places in the United States.

Much research has been directed toward determining whether economically depressed core urban areas are, because of excessive social disorganization, especially prone to suicide. Yet as

TABLE 13—*Rural and Urban Suicide Rates, United States, 1960*

Territorial Categories	Suicide Rate per 100,000 Population
Metropolitan counties	10.6
Urban	10.7
Rural	10.4
Nonmetropolitan counties	10.7
Urban	10.1
Rural	11.0
Total urban	10.5
Total rural	10.8

Source and qualification: Rates computed from suicide data in *Vital Statistics of The United States, 1960*, Vol. II, pt. B, Table 9-9. Census figures for the urban and rural populations have been adjusted (in the way of estimates) to make them correspond to the urban-rural distinction employed in gathering and reporting vital statistics. For all practical purposes, the urban population is restricted to persons residing in incorporated places of 2500 or more inhabitants, which is a much more narrow definition of urban than that employed in the 1960 population census.

From Jack P. Gibbs, "Suicide" in Robert K. Merton and Robert A. Nisbet, *Contemporary Social Problems* (New York: Harcourt, Brace and World, 1966), p. 302.

noted in the preceding chapter, there is considerable evidence that such areas are not especially disorganized, that in many respects social life is highly organized. In this connection, Gibbs and Martin[14] review the research of Schmid,[15] Porterfield[16] and Sainsbury,[17] whose findings indicate definite positive correlations between various measures of geographical population mobility and suicide. Gibbs and Martin state: "If one seeks for a universal common denominator among various suggested empirical referents for the concept of social disorganization, it would appear to be population mobility—generally, residential mobility on the individual level as contrasted with . . . collective migration of groups. . . ."[18] Those authors use six different measures of population mobility and they control by age. They conclude that "mobility varies inversely with suicide rates by age to a remarkable degree."[19] They report rank-difference correlations (p) of —.90 to —.95.

Gibbs and Martin find that when age is taken into account, it is those who are geographically immobile who are most prone to suicide. It may be that people who are on the move are not severely alienated but are to moderate degree caught up in the hustle and bustle, the throb, of everyday life much more than has been thought. It may be, that is, that this transiency involves a middle-range degree of reciprocity. Is it those who do not move who are either enveloped by overreciprocity or bitterly alienated from the social world? Is it perhaps a necessity that individuals remain long in a given social system if tension in that system is to reach extremely high or low levels? These clearly are open and important questions for which we need but do not have even tentative answers.[20]

Findings regarding immigrants to the United States are quite different from those for migrants within the country. Dublin reports that suicide rates for foreign born persons in the United States are significantly higher than for native-born. (See Table 14.) Dublin goes on to say: "These comparisons, however, do not take into consideration the difference in the age distribution of the foreign which is an important factor in the suicidal rate. However, comparison of age adjusted rates, based on a comparable age distribution for the two groups, U.S. and foreign born,

TABLE 14—*Suicide Rates Among the Foreign-Born for Selected Countries of Birth, by Sex, United States, 1959*

	Rates per 100,000*		Ratio to U.S. Rate	
Country of Birth	Males	Females	Males	Females
ALL SELECTED COUNTRIES	35.5	8.7	2.0	1.7
England and Wales	33.7	9.1	1.9	1.8
Ireland	17.9	4.4	1.0	0.9
Norway	42.5	4.0	2.4	0.8
Sweden	56.7	11.0	3.2	2.2
Germany	44.4	11.4	2.5	2.3
Poland	39.3	11.7	2.2	2.3
Czechoslovakia	56.2	10.6	3.2	2.1
Austria	57.8	11.4	3.2	2.3
U.S.S.R.	47.0	14.4	2.6	2.9
Italy	29.7	5.4	1.7	1.1
Canada	31.0	7.5	1.7	1.5
Mexico	12.3	2.6	0.7	0.5

*Crude rates.

Sources: National Office of Vital Statistics, and Bureau of the Census, Department of Commerce.

From Louis I. Dublin, *Suicide* (New York: The Ronald Press, 1963), p. 31.

does not change the picture materially. Foreign born males still have a suicide rate of 35.2 per 100,000, or twice that for all males in the United States, and foreign born females 8.8 per cent per 100,000, or 74 per cent above the rate for all U.S. females."[21]

One might speculate that it is the foreign-born in ghetto-like enclaves in the United States who tend to commit suicide. Those enclaves may be exceedingly close-knit units of high reciprocity and low tension. Again, they may, like black ghettos, involve alternating swings between excessively high and low tension. Suicide may arise also among those foreign-born who have had isolated existences here. Such isolation may indicate alienation and anomie. At the same time, it may mean that the individual of necessity moves in low tension situations simply because his interaction with others is insufficient to generate situations of appreciable tension.[22]

4. *Age and Sex Differences*

Broadly speaking, the relationship between age and suicide is quite the opposite of that between age and homicide. The data in

Table 15 show for the United States a rather clear positive correlation between age and suicide. Only in the very elderly age groups do rates for suicide decline somewhat. Most societies follow this pattern.[23] As Gibbs points out, however, there are societies that in some respects diverge sharply from that pattern.[24] Rates are very low in childhood and adolescence for both Japan and the United States. But the Japanese reach a peak of about 45 per 100,000 of the population in the 20 to 24 age range, drop off, then climb to a rate of about 75 in old age. Altruistic suicide runs high in Japan in early adulthood as does suicide of personal honor. Regarding the latter, loss or threat of loss of prestige is a driving force.[25] Nevertheless, the overall positive relation between suicide and age for the world at large is striking indeed.

TABLE 15—*Suicide Rates for Age Groups by Color and Sex,*
United States, 1960

Age	White			Non-white		
	Male	Female	Total	Male	Female	Total
5- 9	0.0	0.0	0.0	0.0	0.1	0.0
10-14	1.0	0.2	0.6	0.2	0.0	0.1
15-19	5.9	1.6	3.7	3.5	1.5	2.5
20-24	12.0	3.2	7.5	7.4	1.6	4.3
25-29	13.8	4.8	9.2	12.7	3.2	7.6
30-34	15.9	6.8	11.2	13.3	3.9	8.2
35-39	19.6	8.3	13.8	14.6	3.3	8.7
40-44	24.2	8.2	16.1	12.3	4.1	8.0
45-49	30.2	11.0	20.4	12.8	2.7	7.5
50-54	37.6	11.2	24.2	12.2	4.0	8.0
55-59	39.9	10.9	25.1	16.5	3.3	9.8
60-64	40.6	11.2	25.2	17.5	3.0	10.0
65-69	38.5	8.5	22.5	14.0	3.7	8.6
70-74	46.7	9.5	26.6	10.5	3.9	7.0
75-79	52.9	10.0	29.0	5.9	1.8	3.7
80-84	60.9	8.9	31.7	11.3	7.6	11.4
85+	61.4	6.8	27.9	13.1	2.5	7.1
Total	17.6	5.4	11.4	7.1	1.9	4.4

Source: *Vital Statistics of the United States, 1960*, Volume II, Mortality, Office of Vital Statistics (Washington, D.C.), pp. 125-379; *United States Census of Population, 1960: United States Summary, General Population Characteristics*, Bureau of the Census (Washington, D.C.), pp. 159, 160, and 167-72.

From Sanford Labovitz, "Variation in Suicide Rates," in Jack P. Gibbs, *Suicide* (New York: Harper and Row, 1968), p. 64.

As individuals grow older, the social systems in which they move tend to involve greater reciprocity in role relationships. Hence tension in those systems becomes lower. It is in early adulthood that individuals are most often engaged in highly competitive struggles. As the years of the life cycle go on, it is loss of roles that is likely to be a dominant fact. The parental role is lost as offspring grow to adulthood and depart. The marital role is lost through the death of the spouse or through divorce. There is the sheer loss, however obvious, of age roles: youth is lost; young adulthood is lost; middle-age is lost. The economic role is lost through retirement or debilitation.

The individuals who suffer these losses do not for the most part perceive them as due to the aggression machinations of particular others and so do not blame those others. At the same time, the net result is an increasing sterility in role relationship. There is the frustration not only of loss but of the ramifications of that loss. As persons grow older they participate increasingly in stagnating, low tension situations. Suicide is one response. But to what extent so-called normal (non-suicidal) deaths are also responses to this condition goes largely unknown. There is in this regard some evidence that elderly persons who are able to stay on the job, remain dynamically involved with social life and retain their health, while those who retire tend to wither away.[26]

Males commit more suicide, as well as more homicide, than do females. However, the discrepancy is somewhat less great in the case of suicide than homicide. In literate societies, male suicides outnumber female suicides by three and four to one. Table 16 provides rates by sex for 25 literate societies. In none of those countries does the female rate exceed the male rate. The United States rate for males is three-and-a-half times that for females. For a few countries, however, the difference is not especially large. In Iceland, for example, the ratio of male to female rates is 1.3 to 1.0. The analysis of suicide in non-literate societies substantiates the findings for literate societies.[27] Male rates definitely exceed female rates in most of those societies. In a few cases, male rates are about equal to female rates; in none is the female rate greater than that for males.

Males may tend to experience social systems in greater

TABLE 16—*Male and Female Suicide Rates by Countries,* circa *1960**

Country and Year	Suicide Rate per 100,000 Population Male	Female	Ratio of Male to Female Rate	Excess of Male Rate
Australia, 1960	15.0	6.2	2.4	8.8
Austria, 1959	35.8	15.2	2.4	20.6
Belgium, 1959	18.9	7.6	2.5	11.3
Bulgaria, 1960	10.5	4.7	2.2	5.8
Canada, 1960	12.0	3.0	4.0	9.0
Costa Rica, 1960	3.9	0.3	13.0	3.6
Denmark, 1959	28.7	13.5	2.1	15.2
England and Wales, 1959	14.2	8.9	1.6	5.3
Finland, 1960	32.7	8.9	3.7	23.8
France, 1960	24.0	8.2	2.9	15.8
Germany, West, 1960	25.7	12.6	2.0	13.1
Hungary, 1960	35.6	14.9	2.4	20.7
Iceland, 1960	9.0	5.9	1.3	2.1
Italy, 1959	8.9	3.6	2.5	5.3
Japan, 1959	26.6	18.9	1.4	7.7
Luxembourg, 1959	13.4	5.6	2.4	7.8
Netherlands, 1960	8.2	5.1	1.6	3.1
New Zealand, 1959[a]	13.8	4.3	3.2	9.5
Norway, 1959	11.7	4.0	2.9	7.7
Panama, 1960	7.9	2.4	3.3	5.5
Portugal, 1960	13.6	3.7	3.7	9.9
Sweden, 1959	27.2	9.0	3.0	18.2
Switzerland, 1959	30.1	9.4	3.2	20.7
Union of South Africa, 1958[b]	18.9	6.0	3.2	12.9
United States, 1960	16.6	4.7	3.5	11.9

Source: *Demographic Yearbook,* 1961 (New York: United Nations, 1962), Table 19.

[a]European population only.

[b]White population only.

*From Jack P. Gibbs, "Suicide," in Robert K. Merton and Robert A. Nisbet, *Contemporary Social Problems* (New York: Harcourt, Brace and World), 1961, p. 299.

extremes of high and low tension than do females. Males are generally more directly bound up in intense economic activity than are females. In early adulthood they are likely to be engaged in competitive occupational struggle. In some instances, however, they will have by then given up the struggle in despair. In any case, as they grow older, males are more likely than females to suffer the effects of large drops in tension of the social systems in which they participate. Having been in many instances closely involved in high tension social systems, males tend to experience greater shifts to low tension systems than do females. Further, there arises again the question of loss. It is in regard to the economic status-role especially that males as a rule have more to gain and therefore more to lose than females.

5. Race in Relation to Age and Sex

Turning to differences by race, Table 15 shows that rates for whites in the United States are two-and-a-half times those for non-whites, the rates being 11.4 and 4.4 respectively. This of course is in extremely sharp contrast to rates for criminal homicide which are much greater for non-whites than whites. As has been noted, non-whites, the great majority of whom are black in the United States, experience social environments in greater tension than do whites. And they, blacks in particular, suffer the frustration of blockage by others more than do whites, while whites are more subject to role loss by seemingly impersonal means.

However, when one considers age, sex and race in conjunction with one another, a somewhat startling finding is this: While non-white suicide rates are overall quite low compared to white rates, in the years of early adulthood the rates for non-white males are almost as high as for white males. Especially is this true in the 25 to 29 and the 30 to 34 year age brackets. White rates for those periods are respectively 13.8 and 15.9; rates for non-whites are 12.7 and 13.3. Non-white males, mostly black, have extremely high homicide rates during those years but they also show rather high suicide rates.

Evidence recently set forth by Hendin indicates that it is in the black urban ghettos that suicide rates are especially high for males in early adulthood.[28] In the context of the present formulation, this is to be explained largely on these grounds: First, ghetto life is characterized by alternating swings between high and low extremes of situational tension, the high extreme giving rise to· homicide and the low generating suicide. Secondly, considerable numbers of young black males will be subject to the apathy and despair of low tension situations and social systems. This will be so in large measure because of their lack of familial and occupational ties. They have little to do and less hope of doing it. And doing little is likely to mean an environment of low tension.[29]

Looking broadly at age-sex-race categories, these major trends are to be noted: Suicide rates are highest for white males, next highest for non-white males, next for white females, and lowest for non-white females. Homicide rates are greatest for non-white males, next greatest for non-white females, next for white males and least for white females.

Highest suicide rates by far are found among the elderly white males and lowest rates among non-white females in late adolescence and early adulthood. (The rate of 60.9 for white males aged 80 to 84 is 38 times the rate of 1.6 for non-white females in the 20 to 24 age bracket.) In sharp contrast, the lowest rates for homicide are among the middle-aged and elderly white females and the highest rates among the young adult non-white males.

Is it the elderly white males who are most exposed to low tension social systems and the most vulnerable to social loss? Are young adult non-white females least exposed to low tension and loss? Are the young adult non-white males confronted with social systems in both high and low extremes of tension and are middle-aged and older white females the least confronted with those extremes? Although a much greater amount of hard evidence is required, tentative answers to these questions incline toward the affirmative.

6. *Variations by Prestige Groupings*

While there is a definite inverse correlation between homicide and occupational prestige, the relationship between suicide and occupational prestige is decidely less clear. On the surface, at least, suicide rates increase as extremes of high and low occupational prestige are reached and are lowest in occupations of middle range prestige. Labovitz draws together data that tend to support this generalization. (See Table 17.) A number of reports show the same general result.[30]

Numerous exceptions can be found, however, especially when

TABLE 17—*Suicide Rates by Occupational Groups, United States (1950), Los Angeles (1965), and Tulsa (1937-1956 Average)*

Occupation	U.S. Males (20-64)	LOS ANGELES Males	Females	Total	Tulsa
Professional	21.7	23.7	15.2	21.0	35.1
Managers	28.5	22.2	23.0	22.3	
Clerical	16.6	18.1	10.4	13.5	11.6
Sales	24.7	18.1	10.4	13.5	11.6
Craftsmen	26.7	19.7	8.7	17.7	14.3
Operatives	21.3				20.5
Service workers	29.7	14.7	3.3	10.0	23.9
Laborers	32.8				
Farmers and farm laborers	35.1				
Unemployed		76.6	52.9	68.2	
Total Employed	26.0				

Sources: National Office of Vital Statistics, *Vital Statistics—Special Reports*, Vol. 53, No. 3 (September, 1963); data for Los Angeles are from Michael L. Peck, Suicide Prevention Center, Los Angeles, California. These data are from the County Coroner. Occupational titles were matched to those used in the census and the population size of each occupation was estimated from data in the 1960 census. Data for Tulsa are from Elwin H. Powell, "Occupation, Status, and Suicide: Toward a Redefinition of Anomie," *American Sociological Review*, 23 (April, 1958), p. 135.

From Sanford Labovitz, "Variation in Suicide Rates," in Jack P. Gibbs, *Suicide* (New York: Harper and Row, 1968), p. 70.

more specific occupations are investigated.[31] College professors possess a low suicide rate as do electrical engineers; dentists have a high rate.[32] Pharmacists possess a high rate (120.0); and so also do cab drivers (86.9). Accountants have a fairly low rate (7.0); and the rate for carpenters is lower (5.0).[33]

Dublin reports on Great Britain as follows:[34] "One of the most striking features of the recent British reports is the finding that certain groups of professional workers have the highest rates registered. These include physicians, dentists, barristers, and solicitors—intellectuals who work under some degree of nervous pressure. These men witness much human maladjustment and suffering of one kind or another. High suicide mortality among physicians and dentists probably results in part also from constant occupational contact with convenient means of suicide. Other professional workers in this class, however, such as teachers, have low rates and clergymen of certain denominations stand near the bottom of the entire list. Rates greatly above average are recorded for persons engaged in various lines of liquor trade and indicate an established relationship between suicide and alcoholism. Other occupational groups showing unusually high mortality from suicide are auctioneers and appraisers, wholesale and retail dealers, makers of watches and scientific instruments, commercial travelers, insurance agents, and bank and insurance clerks. Farm laborers show an average mortality. Exceptionally low mortality is found among groups of railway workers and officials, bargemen and boatmen, chemical workers, civil service officials and clerks, and various building trade workers."[35]

In an interesting research note, Alpert provides data that indicate a strong association of suicide with higher socio-economic groups and homicide with lower socio-economic groups. He draws on statistics regarding the deaths of holders of ordinary and of industrial life insurance. As Alpert says, "The latter, it is generally known, belong to lower socio-economic groups than the former." For the period 1942 to 1949 in the United States, those in the higher prestige group had suicide rates twice as high as those in the lower group. And those in the lower group had homicide death rates three times those in the upper group.[36]

7. *Downward Mobility*

But to turn now to the critical question of downward social mobility and suicide: Breed's New Orleans study of 103 white male suicides and 206 control subjects, matched for sex, race, and age bears directly on the question.[37] Breed found that suicides tended to come from the lower occupational prestige groups more often than did the controls (who closely paralleled occupational data for all white males in the city). Three times as many suicides as controls were in the lower strata and only three-fifths as many were in the upper strata. Regarding mobility, Breed's results show that the suicides' occupational prestige was higher than that of their fathers in only 25 per cent of the cases as compared to 38 per cent for the controls. The suicides' occupational prestige was lower than the fathers' in 53 per cent of the cases as compared to 31 per cent for the control group.

Based on the North-Hatt categories of occupational prestige, Breed's results show that 33 per cent of the suicides who were employed full-time and 50 per cent of the suicides who were not employed full-time were downwardly mobile; these figures are in striking contrast to the five per cent of the controls who were downwardly mobile. (See Table 18.) On the other hand, the suicides were slightly more upwardly mobile than the controls; 17 per cent of the suicides employed full-time and nine per cent of those employed part-time were upwardly mobile as compared to 12 per cent of the controls. The upwardly mobile suicides were likely to be in the more prestigious occupations. However, Breed found that it was the suicide victims in these occupations, as compared to the victims in other occupational prestige groups, who had experienced the highest rate of income loss prior to suicide. That is to say, these men tended to be failing in relation to the society's success goals even though they still retained their relatively prestigious occupations. And in a more general sense, Breed reports an enormous difference between income gain and loss over the two years preceding the suicides for the entire suicidal group as compared to the control group.

TABLE 18—*Worklife Mobility of Working and Non-Working Suicides and Controls, Using Two Occupational Scales—Per Cent**

	SUICIDES		
		Not	
Work Status	*Full-time*	*Full-time*	*Controls*
Using Census categories			
Upward	19	9	12
Same (or only 1 job)	57	45	83
Downward	24	47	5
Using North-Hatt categories			
Upward	17	9	12
Same (or only 1 job)	50	41	83
Downward	33	50	5
Totals	52	51	187

*The worklife comparison for the suicides is between last job held and the one preceding. For the controls the comparison was restricted to the past 10-year period; more mobility in both directions would have been shown had a longer work period been studied.

From Warren Breed, "Occupational Mobility and Suicide among White Males," *American Sociological Review* (April, 1963), pp. 178-88.

Income decreased for 51 per cent of the suicides and 11 per cent
of the controls; it increased for eight per cent of the suicides and
35 per cent of the controls; income remained the same for 41 per
cent of the suicide group and 54 per cent of the control group.[38]

Taking Breed's study as a whole, the conclusions are inescap-
able that in his samples, suicides were "failures" in terms of
societal goals, were "losers" in relation to their fathers and in
relation to what they themselves had earlier achieved occupa-
tionally. The findings tend to clarify to some extent the moderate
confusion that exists as to whether suicide is associated with
both high and low extremes of occupational prestige or with the
latter only:[39] Those suicidal individuals in the lower strata frequently arrived there by moving down the occupational prestige
hierarchy.[40] Those in the higher strata would seem often to be
on the verge of such downward movement.

8. *Motives, Methods, Places, Times*

Hendin lists six major motives for suicide:[41] retroflexed murder, that is, murder of another turned against the self; reunion
with a loved one; rebirth of the self after death; self-punishment;
seeing oneself as already dead; and retaliatory abandonment, that
being when the suicidal victim abandons forever one who has
abandoned him. Dublin suggests the following as precipitating
motivations in suicide: ill health, fear of insanity, disappointment
in love, illicit sex-relations, belief that life is futile, hopeless
poverty, unemployment, altruism, and greed.[42]

In the author's study of non-literate societies, three major types
of motives were ascribed to suicidal individuals by other members of the society: self-condemnation, fear, and anger toward
others, the first two being decidedly the most prevalent.[43]
Everything considered, these various motives reflect frustration,
especially over interpersonal losses, consequent aggression and,
to a lesser degree, self-blame.

Shooting, hanging, cutting, poisoning, gassing, drowning,
jumping from heights are among literate societies nearly universal
methods of committing suicide.[44] Percentage distributions for
major methods for four time periods since 1901 in the United

States are provided by Dublin in Table 19. Firearms and explosives have over the century replaced poisons and gas as the leading means of death.[45]

Table 20 shows that in the United States males use firearms and explosives over half of the time, hanging and strangulation a fifth of the time and poisoning and asphyxiation a sixth of the time. In contrast, poisoning and asphyxiation are the leading methods for females, employed in a third of suicidal cases. Firearms and explosives are used by females a quarter of the time and hanging and strangulation slightly over a fifth of the time. As is true for homicide, females, less familiar than males with the use of firearms, tend more than males to employ other means.

There is considerable variation in method from one society to another. Methods most common in Canada, Australia, and New Zealand, are similar to the United States. However, in England and Scotland, the most usual methods in descending order of frequency are poisoning, gassing, hanging, drowning; firearms are infrequently used. In Denmark poisoning is the most frequent form of self-killing while in Sweden it is hanging; firearms are seldom employed in either country.[46] In a sample of 54 non-literate societies, hanging, poisoning, drowning, and jumping from high places were common methods.[47] The use of weapons

TABLE 19—*Percentage Distribution of Deaths from Suicide, by Specified Method*

U.S. Registration Area 1901-1905, 1911-1915; U.S. Registration States 1926-1930; and Total U.S. 1955-1959

Method	1955-1959	1926-1930	1911-1919	1901-1905
Firearms and explosives	47.1	35.1	30.0	24.4
Poisons and gases	20.8	31.1	39.9	42.1
Hanging and strangulation	20.5	18.1	14.6	15.0
Cutting or piercing instruments	2.6	5.4	6.4	5.7
Drowning	3.7	5.2	5.6	5.1
Jumping from high places	3.5	3.1	1.9	1.2
Other unspecified	1.9	2.0	1.6	6.5

Source: National Office of Vital Statistics.
From Louis I. Dublin, *Suicide* (New York: The Ronald Press, 1963), p. 38.

TABLE 20—*Percentage Distribution of Deaths from Suicide by Specified Method or Means Among White Men and Women in Given Age Groups, United States, 1955-1959*

Method	AGE GROUPS				
	All Ages	*10-24*	*25-44*	*45-64*	*65 & over*
White Males					
Firearms and explosives	53.3	53.8	54.6	53.1	52.0
Poisoning and asphyxiation	17.3	18.4	2.31	17.8	9.9
Hanging and strangulation	20.0	22.5	14.8	19.7	25.8
All others	9.4	5.3	7.4	9.4	12.3
White Females					
Firearms and explosives	24.9	43.8	32.9	20.9	12.6
Poisoning and asphyxiation	34.6	32.4	37.7	35.5	27.0
Hanging and strangulation	22.6	12.0	15.9	25.4	32.7
All others	17.6	11.7	13.5	18.2	27.8

Source: National Office of Vital Statistics.
From Louis I. Dublin, *Suicide* (New York: The Ronald Press, 1963), p. 41.

—knives, spears, firearms—was unusual although these were in general available.

While homicide occurs in or near the home to a considerable degree, Pokorney found that suicide takes place in the home to an even greater extent. Of 91 suicides in Houston, Texas, 76 per cent were carried out in the home. Of 438 homicides in that city, 42 per cent occurred in the home.[48] At the same time, suicide is a solitary act; others are rarely present when it occurs.[49] Pokorney's results showed also that homicide and suicide tended to take place in different areas of the city. There was a correlation coefficient of but .12 between census tracts in which suicidal and homicidal victims lived.[50]

Studies of the time of year at which suicide occurs present a somewhat confused picture. Pokorney found no particular patterns by month or season.[51] Dublin reports that in 1960 in the United States, the highest rates were in the second quarter of the year, in April in particular, while the lowest were in the third quarter, especially December.[52] Dublin states that similar variations obtain for England and Wales and for Vienna.[53] On the other hand, Schmid found that male suicide rates in Minneapolis were greatest in January and February.[54] In any event homicide tends to predominate in the summer months and suicide does not.

In contrast to homicide, which is most prevalent on weekends, suicide rates are highest during the middle of the week. Schmid in the Minneapolis study found suicide rates were highest on Tuesdays and lowest on Saturdays.[55] Pokorney reports that in Houston the highest suicide rates were on Thursdays while Fridays and Saturdays had the lowest rates; for homicide, Wednesday was the low day and Saturday the high.[56] Suicide and homicide contrast also in regard to the time of day at which death occurs. Suicide is most usual in the late morning and early afternoon and homicide shortly before or after midnight.[57] It is quiet when suicide occurs, loud when homicide takes place.

Looking back over the data presented in this chapter, there is indicated a clear tendency for suicide to arise in social systems and situations in low tension and in those where tension has decreased in large measure. The individual counterparts of this are inner role systems in low tension, severe drops in inner tension, and feelings of apathy and loss. It is to considerations of this that the discussion now turns.

CHAPTER VII

Suicide, the Individual and Social Control

1. *Inner Role Systems*

The inner role system of the individual is in low tension when he perceives little interference among performances in his various roles. As tension grows very low, it seems to the given individual from a rational standpoint that the smoothness of inner organization approximates the ideal. Yet he feels an inexplicable and severe frustration. The lack of perceived pull of one performance against another means disintegration of the personality. The tension that provides support of inner space, so to speak, hardly exists; tension is so weak that the self verges on, and in fact may, collapse.

This is not a common phenomenon in the Western world at least, and in the United States in particular. The vaguely comprehended terrors of inner low tension are so great that men will go to desperate lengths to avoid such a condition. That avoidance is the subject of consideration at future points in the discussion.

The individual's perception of lack of interference among his role performances and of decreases in that interference will depend largely on several variables. It will depend on the extent to which others facilitate through reciprocity his performances such that the time and energy he devotes to one do not interfere with execution of another. And the perception of interference depends also on the number of roles the individual performs. Other things equal, the smaller is the number of roles, the less the interference. Generally the fewer roles the individual has performed in the past and the more others have reciprocated toward him, the less is he likely to perceive interferences among his performances now.[1]

When inner tension grows very low, the foundations of inner belief are drastically shaken.[2] That seeming inner peace and

127

harmony which the individual has held as an ideal, turn out in practice to be extremely disturbing. If tension in the inner system has been consistently low, the individual suffers continually a collapsed internal state, an inner nothingness. And yet these matters are not understood by him. If tension in the inner system cannot be sufficiently increased, then blame for a disastrous condition must be fixed. Since the social environment surrounding the individual seems to him really quite optimal, the self suffers the blame. In one sense the self is the frustrator of itself and so becomes a target of the consequent aggression. For if the individual were able to change his perceptions of his performances, inner tension would then increase and frustration would decrease.

When the individual seeks, unwittingly or otherwise, to raise tension in his inner system, he is likely to attempt to rearrange the environment so that it becomes in fact more difficult for him to carry out his performances. He can do this by reciprocating less toward others. If they then in turn reciprocate less toward him, his performances will become more demanding. Of course, he may be reluctant initially to decrease his reciprocity toward others for they are reciprocating toward him.

But there will be a further possibility. The individual may increase significantly his already great reciprocity toward others. This may threaten them with conditions of severely low tension in social system and situations sufficiently that they reduce their reciprocity toward him. They may, that is, out of desperation react aggressively to his attempts "to kill with kindness." If so, the individual now will experience more difficulty in carrying out his performances. He is likely to perceive that and to view his performances as interfering more than previously with each other. Thus tension in the inner system will rise. If this occurs, he is then in a position to begin to blame others for his "difficulties." He will in the process have moved away to some degree from the horrors of low tension and self-blame.

2. *Loss of Love Objects*

Loss of prestige as a variable in suicide has been mentioned. In particular, downward occupational mobility and suicide have been discussed. Frequently, loss and low tension in social systems and in inner status and role systems coexist. For example, skid road inhabitants have lost occupational prestige standing. So also, although in quite a different way, have male residents of retirement villages. Both sit in the stagnation of low environmental tension.

More than others suicidal persons have experienced the loss of individuals close to them. About half of those who commit suicide lost in childhood one or both parents through divorce, separation, or death. This is in contrast to estimates of 17 to 33 per cent for the general population.[3] Dorpat *et al.* summarize research on such losses as follows:[4] "This study reports on broken homes in childhood as related to the suicidal behavior of an unselected and consecutive series of 114 subjects who completed suicide and a series of 121 subjects who attempted suicide in King County, Wash. Fifty per cent of the subjects who completed suicide and 64 per cent of those subjects who attempted suicide came from broken homes. The incidence of death of a parent was highest for the completed suicide group and was the most common cause of a broken home. In contrast, the most important cause of a broken home in childhood for the attempted suicide group was divorce, the incidence being significantly higher than in the completed suicide group. Almost half of those who had come from broken homes in the completed suicide group had lost both parents; whereas, nearly two thirds of those who had broken homes in the attempted suicide group has lost both parents. This research supports the theories of Bowlby and Zilboorg that parental loss in childhood predisposes to depression and suicide later in life. The recent loss of a love object was a frequent precipitating factor in both the attempted and the completed suicide groups. It is hypothesized that unresolved object loss in childhood leads to an inability to sustain object losses in later life. This in turn leads to depressive reactions culminating in suicide behavior."

Further, suicides have lost mother or father or both in adulthood to a much larger extent than the general population; the respective percentages are of the order of 45 for suicides and 20 for others.[5] Rushing reports that 27 per cent of a group of suicides lost a family member in the years immediately preceding their death and many more lost some "love-object" individual outside the family shortly before suicide.[6]

Moreover, suicides have frequently experienced disruption of social relations from other sources. Many have been living alone prior to suicide—perhaps as high a percentage as 25 compared to seven per cent for the population in general.[7] Granting that the word of those who attempt suicide may be questioned, Rushing cites two studies that bear on the matter. In one, about half of the subjects stated that the "main reason" for the attempt was friction with someone close to them. In the other study, 37 per cent pointed to various types of disruptions in social relations as the major reason for attempting suicide.[8]

When individuals have lost others close to them, whether parents, spouses, or friends, certain roles are also of necessity gone. There are no sons without fathers, no wives without husbands. Situational tension is, other things equal, necessarily reduced. There is no unreciprocity without interaction. There is much evidence that because of such losses, especially in early life, suicidal persons are overly dependent individuals.[9] They need the assurance of others so greatly that in their desperate demands for it they may drive others away from them, thereby closing the door to help.

When loss or absence of the marital status and role—single, married, divorced, widowed—are considered in conjunction with suicide, it is well to control for age. On the one hand, there is the variation of suicide by age *per se*; on the other, some age groups are not compatible with a given status and role, as childhood is not with marriage. Table 21 shows rates by age, and marital status and role for the United States for 1959. The divorced have the greatest suicide rate, the widowed the next greatest, the single next and the married the lowest rate. In particular, rates are highest for divorced males in middle or old age, next highest for widowed males of all adult ages and next for elderly single males. Rates for females, although low by male standards, follow roughly the same relative patterns.

These differences are significant. They point to the loss of marital roles through divorce or death of the spouse as a factor

TABLE 21—*Mortality from Suicide by Marital Status and Age Groups Men and Women 15 Years and Over, United States, 1959*

		MALES			
Age Group	Total	Single	Married	Widowed	Divorced
15-24	7.4	6.8	8.4	—	19.7
25-34	14.5	23.2	11.1	95.8	66.7
35-44	20.5	29.8	16.7	81.7	112.6
45-54	30.3	39.0	25.6	58.3	111.7
55-64	39.1	58.3	32.4	65.0	89.4
65-74	45.5	82.0	33.6	79.6	152.5
75 and over	54.6	85.3	34.5	79.2	140.0
		FEMALES			
15-24	2.1	1.7	2.4	—	12.4
25-34	5.5	9.2	4.7	7.2	17.8
35-44	6.9	9.4	5.9	10.2	24.4
45-54	8.5	8.8	7.5	12.0	17.4
55-64	9.8	12.3	8.0	12.4	19.6
65-74	9.7	9.6	7.5	11.3	25.8
75 and over	6.4	4.0	4.6	6.9	18.4

From Louis I. Dublin, *Suicide: A Sociological and Statistical Study* (New York: The Ronald Press, 1963), p. 27. Source: National Office of Vital Statistics, unpublished data.

of much importance in suicide and especially so for men. Apart from the sheer loss of a role, the dissolution of a marriage generally means a loss of support for both partners or for the surviving spouse. That support may take the obvious form of providing comfort for the other spouse. However, it may take an opposite form: the support that is a consequence of unreciprocity between spouses. Marital partners may grow used to, and come to depend on, daily fighting, arguing, bickering. Again, support may be a combination of these two diverse forms.

Over his life history, the suicidal person has suffered one severe social loss and then another—of persons and of roles especially. He is vulnerable to loss because he has lost so much. His hurt, his frustration, is great. Moreover, he has lost role models: a parent or grandparent, an older sibling, a friend. He has had the models but some of them have abruptly departed. His world is likely to be a mixture of what seems to him extremes of stability and instability. His environment—both external and internal—is one of considerable harmony punctuated by either inexplicable or impersonal losses. The death of someone close may be inexplicable. The lay-off from the job or the retirement may be impersonal in the sense all in a given seniority group are laid off, all in a given age-group are retired.

The suicidal person tests his precarious environment frequently. He tries to ascertain whether or not significant others will be there tomorrow. It is his conception of the world, based on very good personal evidence, that other persons on whom one might depend can disappear from one moment to the next. Thus he tests, seeks total commitment from others, to insure that they will be there tomorrow. If they will be, he will be. But he cannot know with any certainty that they will be there. His compulsive search for absolute commitment from other individuals can on the one hand never find fulfillment for no one possesses the means for making such a total commitment. On the other hand, in his attempt he is likely to drive others further from him, to create a loss where there was none.

3. *Identity*

The smothering atmosphere of low tension in the inner system and in surrounding social systems stunts the development of identity. When the social system is dominant and placid and the inner system reflects that placidity there is no way that identity can blossom. One might as well attempt to grow flowers in a vacuum. The process of growth of identity is slowed and in some cases reversed by the occurrence of severe, highly personal losses. Identity is built upon the reactions of others.[10] When they are gone, the sense of self is quickly lost.

If inner tension is very low, there obtains a one-dimensional identity that lacks versimilitude, that possesses the grinding sameness of one performance played over and over. For the perceived absence of interference among role performances leads those performances to become, from the individual's subjective standpoint, fused into one. If inner tension grows exceedingly low—if performances are perceived as pulling against each other hardly at all—the framework for the self collapses and identity lies like a deflated balloon upon the floor of the mind. If over the life history tension has been low continually, then there will have been an insufficiently rounded framework upon which to develop that dynamic sense of self-recognition which is identity.

Attempts at suicide are in part the means of trying to recapture a lost identity or to build a new identity. While many of those who commit suicide are not known to have made previous attempts, attempts have been made by a much higher proportion of those who actually commit suicide than by the general population.[11] In one study, Shneidman *et al.* found that 75 per cent of suicidal victims either attempted or threatened suicide.[12] Kobler and Stotland state that a majority of those who take their own lives have told others of the possibility.[13] And Rushing reports that 29 per cent of suicides previously made verbal threats that they would kill themselves.[14] In many of these cases, either of oral communication or of actual attempts at death, the suicidal individuals have by their behavior tried to communicate to others the likelihood of impending disaster, the need for help, their desperate search for identity; and they have failed.

The completed suicidal act is itself not infrequently a last attempt to gain identity.[15] The individual may believe firmly that by his violent act he will create a new life, a new identity, for himself. He imagines he will cut all ties with the past and after the cleansing rite of suicide begin again (although often with the same people he has known previously). He takes control of his destiny. And he does in fact gain a certain identity, that of a suicide. As he is in the coffin and then in the grave, others speak of his various qualities: "He never complained." "He seemed more cheerful of late." "He had everything to live for." And by their hushed tones and studied avoidance of explicit statement of suicide they affix to him more firmly and permanently the label of suicide than could be done by direct means. He remains indefinitely the member of the family who killed himself.

Viewed from one perspective, it is in great part the enormous threat to identity of low levels of tension in the inner or social system or both that drives the fear of that low tension. How does one grapple with, and fashion a self out of, a vacuum? These are the questions which the individual asks himself, however vaguely, or which he feels and senses rather than asks.

It is certainly difficult, individuals feel, to exist with the wracking strains of high tension. Yet there are others who can be blamed and attacked. Under low tension conditions, the individual thrashes in a sea of reciprocity (or the absence of unreciprocity), is internally supported by nothing, and blames the self. The suicidal act can also be construed, then, as an extreme attempt to roil the placid waters of low tension.

4. Reaction-formation and Delusion

The threat of low levels of tension can loom so large that a phobic reaction-formation to those levels develops. It is ordinarily exceedingly difficult and therefore rare for an individual to change in a significant degree the wider social environment surrounding him. He can, however, change his inner system by shifting his perceptions of his performances. This is where delusion, mania, and depression may assume a special relevance.

The individual forced into a corner, so to speak, by the unseen terrors of low tension and with no effective way of coping with his environment may turn as a last resort to delusion. Gradually he may perceive his few readily performed social roles as interfering with one another more and more. He may come to see other persons as reciprocating less and thus to see them as the source of the imagined interference among his performances. There is likely here, of course, to be a self-fulfilling prophecy. Others are "put off" by the individual's delusionary symptoms. They avoid him[16] and they withhold their reciprocity.

The individual's delusions will often be sufficient in themselves, however, to raise tension in his inner system to a high level and to effect thereby a reaction-formation to low tension. He experiences the frustration of the severe shock that is a consequence of a sudden large increase in tension. He seeks now to avoid high inner tension. He turns again to delusion. He envisages his performances as growing rapidly easier, as interfering with one another less and less. He views others as being more helpful, more reciprocating. Inner tension decreases and once again approaches a very low level. A further phobic reaction sets in and so the pendulum swings. In the course of that process, delusion feeds on delusion.

It is out of these conditions that manic-depression can readily grow. If a person is to believe in the manic phase that he is able to accomplish near miracles and in the depressive phase that he is totally worthless, it will be necessary that he distort the world including himself through widely contrasting sets of persistent false beliefs.

While delusion, depression, and mania are by no means inevitable concomitants of suicide, they are present in at least a considerable number of cases. Percentages of suicidal victims diagnosed as depressed psychotics range in various studies from six to 45.[17] As Rushing points out, "Follow-up studies of depressed psychotics reveal extremely high suicide rates. In one set of five studies, the average per cent is 14.5. . . ."[18] Manic-depressive psychotics have especially high suicide rates. One tabulation gives an annual suicide rate of 87.4 per 100,000 resident hospital patients diagnosed as manic-depressive. For those with involutional disorders the rate is 80.4; for dementia praecox patients, 30.1. For the overall hospital population the rate is 34.0.[19]

Obviously many severely depressed persons do not commit suicide. And many suicide victims have not had histories of depression. One the one hand it can be said with assurance that aggression directed inward whether because of social loss, excessive reciprocity or otherwise, tends to generate depression.[20] And seriously depressed individuals are more prone to suicide than most others. Nonetheless, it cannot be said with any validity that a prolonged depressive state is a necessary condition for suicide.

As is well known the excessive use of alcohol can serve to further delusion.[21] Schmidt *et al.* found that of patients admitted to a St. Louis hospital, chronic alcoholics were good risks not to commit suicide.[22] One the other hand, however, a number of studies report 21, 20, 11, 8, 8, and 7 per cent of alcoholics commit suicide.[23] The percentages of suicidal victims found to be alcoholics have ranged in various reports from 31, to 30, to 23, to 10 to 6.[24]

5. *Homicide Followed by Suicide*

It is in homicide and suicide by the same individual that one sees the pendulum swings of reaction formation on a large scale. There is violence at either extreme. Beginning usually with the threat of severe low tension, delusion leads the individual to escalate inner tension and to blame one or more others for his plight. Those others become the targets of outward aggression when tension reaches a very high level. In the aftermath of violence (usually directed at someone close to him), the offender plunges toward the nadir of inner tension. Rather than suffer the depths of depression and in the face of the loss of a loved one by his own hand, he kills himself.

In relation to homicide alone, some societies have much homicide-suicide, others relatively little. The United States is in the latter category. Guttmacher reports that in Baltimore six per cent of those who murdered later killed themselves.[25] Wolfgang found in the Philadelphia study that four per cent of the offenders committed suicide shortly after committing homicide. Durrett and Stronguist put the figure at two per cent for several cities in the South.[26] In sharp contrast, Siciliano's research on homicide in Denmark gives the finding of 42 per cent.[27] And the percentage in England is about 33.[28]

One of the most extensive researches of homicide followed by suicide is the English study by D. J. West.[29] He compared a sample of 148 homicidal-suicidal cases with a sample of 148 homicidal cases. In both groups about half of the offenders were judged to be suffering psychological abnormalities—especially depressive disorders—to such an extreme extent that the juries' findings were of insanity or diminished responsibility.[30] The occupational prestige of homicide-suicide offenders was remarkably similar to that of the general population while the homicidal group show a distinct preponderance of individuals in the lower prestige strata.[31]

In the same study, offenders and victims in homicide-suicide cases were found to be familially related significantly more often than in homicide alone.[32] Suicidal offenders tended to kill more than one victim more often than other offenders. Multiple victims were more likely to be family members than single victims; and they were especially likely to be the offenders' children.[33] All in all, homicide-suicide was found to be largely a domestic affair: Of the 148 cases, 53 mothers killed their children; 62 fathers killed their children; and three women killed their husbands or lovers.

Forty-one per cent of the offenders in West's homicide-suicide sample were females in contrast to but 12 per cent of the homicidal cases.[34] Young offenders were more common in the homicide cases than in the homicide-suicide cases: 49 per cent of the homicidal offenders were under age 30 as compared to 18 per cent of the homicide-suicide offenders.[35] However, females who committed both homicide and suicide tended to be younger than females who committed homicide only.[36] Fewer of the homicide-suicide offenders had previous criminal records than the purely homicidal offenders.[37] Gas, poisoning and shooting were the major methods in the homicide-suicide cases and were more prevalent than in the homicide cases. Both types of cases tended to take place late at night.[38] Homicides occurred most frequently on Saturdays and homicide-suicides on Mondays.[39]

Wolfgang found that white homicidal offenders committed suicide more frequently than black offenders. "Although whites are one-fourth of all offenders, they *significantly* make up half of the homicide-suicides."[40] He found also that "males comprise 83 per cent of all homicide offenders, but make up 22 of the 24 homicide-suicides."[41] He states, "Of all homicides, half of the victims were killed violently; whereas among homicide-suicide cases three quarters met death violently...."[42]

As for the part played by alcohol, Wolfgang notes "Alcohol was present in the homicide situation in the Philadelphia study in as many as 6 or 7 out of 10 homicides in general, but in only 3 out of 10 homicides followed by suicide.... Perhaps the lower incidence of alcohol in homicide-suicide situations indicates a greater likelihood of premeditation by the offender."[43] Regarding arrest records: "One-third of homicide-suicide offenders have a previous arrest record compared to nearly two-thirds of all offenders."[44] As for age of the Philadelphia offenders, Wolfgang says this: "The median age of those who committed suicide (38.3 years) is about 7 years *older* than that for all offenders (31.9

years), while the median age of victims of the homicide-suicide group (30.1 years) is about 5 years *younger* than that for all victims (35.1 years)."[45] Finally, Wolfgang states that in Philadelphia the proportion of close personal attachments between offenders who committed suicide and their victims was significantly higher than between other offenders and victims.[46]

Broadly speaking, the findings of West in England, of Wolfgang in Philadelphia—and of Siciliano in Denmark as well—are similar. West concludes, "As far as they go, the statistics available in these three communities all fit the hypothesis that murderers who kill themselves, compared with murderers in general, form a less socially deviant group, and that their relationships to their victims are more often close and intimate."[47]

In homicide-suicide cases there is an escalation of unreciprocity between homicidal victim and offender. Once they reciprocated; now they do the opposite. Upon the death of the victim, the offender finds himself suffering loss because of that death, finds himself no longer with an opponent, finds himself shrouded in apathy.

6. *Social Control and Self-fulfilling Prophecy*

As is the case with homicide, the society does little of a basic preventive nature in regard to suicide. While action is taken, often abortively, when individuals signal in one way or another that they are contemplating suicide, almost nothing is done prior to that. The social control process deals hardly at all with those forces in the social system that give rise to suicide. And it deals not in any significant degree with individuals who have suicidal tendencies but are as yet far from overt self-violence.

An exceedingly fine line exists between attempts to help the potentially suicidal person which, however well meant, increase his conception of himself as suicidal and those responses which do in fact lessen the likelihood of suicide. If others respond to suicidal threats with actions that serve to reduce the individuals' sense of stagnation and loss, then the likelihood of actual suicide will tend to decrease. If others respond with indifference or in ways that increase stagnation and loss, then the chances of suicide grow greater.[48] When indications of impending suicide are met with a labeling of the individual as dangerous to himself, as a suicide risk, then he is likely to take on the identity of a suicide. Self-fulfilling prophecy may well prevail and the likelihood of suicide may be increased.[49]

Everything considered, the evidence is strong that in the United States the social control process tends to affix to the individual who gives any small sign of killing himself the label of suicide and so to increase the probability that he will kill himself. Bennett argues that all depressed persons are potential suicides and should be treated as such.[50] He adds that physical complaints without true organic symptoms mean the diagnostician should look for depression.[51] Suicidal attempts, Bennett believes, should always be followed by definitive psychiatric treatment.[52] He holds also that suicide frequently occurs when the patient is on the way to recovery and that relatives should be warned of this.[53] In conjunction with that approach and referring to depressed subjects, Shneidman cautions: "A good rule is that any significant change in behavior, even if it looks like improvement, should be assessed as a possible prodromal index for suicide."[54]

Shneidman and Farberow emphasize and reemphasize the need for "watchfulness"; "Physicians and relatives must be especially cautious and watchful for at least ninety days after a person who has been suicidal appears to be improving."[55] Further, "The person who threatens suicide seems to be more emotionally disturbed than the person who attempts suicide, but both must be taken seriously and watched carefully for at least three months."[56] When physicians, nurses, ward attendants, and relatives are watchful regarding suicide attempts, it is a near certainty that they will indicate to the individual by small or large cues that they consider him suicidal, thus very likely increasing his identity as a potential suicide victim.

An extreme example of labeling of individuals as suicidal is provided by Bennett. He writes: "In the Berkeley, California Police Department, for example, all statements about suicide are treated as if the person were attempting to commit suicide, and he is talked to in private or his family is advised to take him to one of two hospitals or to his family physician for consultation.

Police officers feel that all such persons should have the benefit of expert advice."[57]

And an unusual process of selecting individuals for labeling is delineated by Shneidman *et al.*: "The primary type of person seen by the SPC (Suicide Prevention Center, Los Angeles), although other types are also seen, is a person who has made a serious suicide attempt and who is hospitalized on the wards of the Los Angeles County General Hospital (LACGH) for medical or surgical treatment as a result of the suicidal behavior." Then, "By and large, persons who have attempted suicide are selected by the SPC for help and for study on the basis of duplicating proportionally the characteristics (as to sex, age, race, religion, socioeconomic distribution, etc.) of the total group of suicide *attempters* in Los Angeles County."[58] The "processing of a subject" by SPC, as it is termed, consists of gathering data about the individual; referral to another agency, to an institution, to a therapist, or occasionally to the SPC itself; and a follow-up to this.[59]

Hospitalization of those thought to be suicidal, surveillance of them, removal of objects believed to be employable as a means of death are usual. Overreaction of professional personnel is not uncommon. As Litman and Farberow point out: "Professional persons sometimes express an exaggerated or disproportionate degree of anxiety over a relatively mild self-destructive communication from a patient or client."[60]

Overreciprocity of institutional personnel alternates with underreciprocity. Referring to patients who appear to wish to control their own destinies by suicide, Shneidman writes: "The nurse can play a life saving role with such a person by recognizing his psychological problems and by enduring his controlling (and irritating) behavior—indeed, by being the walking target of his berating and demanding behavior and thus permitting him to expend his energies in this way, rather than in suicidal activities . . . this can be a difficult role continually to fulfill."[61] Such altruistic endeavor may be difficult for the patient as well as for the nurse. The patient may well be seeking a life-giving aggressive interchange rather than a passive target.

Moss and Hamilton[62] report with approval that when a group of individuals who had attempted suicide were provided with psychotherapy, 22 per cent killed themselves. The figure is actually higher than in several studies where therapy was not received.[63] It was believed by Moss and Hamilton that "therapy was often lifesaving."[64] It was further believed that in the course of therapy there was a period—after substantial progress had been made—when suicide was especially likely to occur. This was a time when the patient tended to make a "flight into reality," away from the hospital and back into an environment with which he could not cope. Relatives of the patient were to be warned of this and "coached" on what to do. Thus, the identity of the patient as a potential suicide was communicated to him by therapists and family members alike.

Patients in the Moss and Hamilton study were observed at every turn. Those authors state: "Constant observation, necessarily invading every privacy, by a nursing staff who functioned as companions and not just as guards, was an absolute necessity with the seriously suicidal patient."[65] On the one hand, this provides the patient with interactional situations in which he can take part. Thus he is spared the frustration of sitting hour after hour in what amounts to solitary confinement. On the other hand, being constantly observed clearly implies to the patient that he is quite definitely a prospect for suicide.

In contrast to the approach used in the cases reported by Moss and Hamilton, Wilmer argues strongly for providing "suicidal patients" in a therapeutic community with firm expectations that they will not commit suicide. He reports positive results.[66] As Wilmer says: "The practice of writing 'suicidal precautions' orders on patients' charts . . . is not only ineffectual but has some very unfortunate results. . . . The doctor goes home. They (the staff) are left with the orders, the responsibility and the patient. They tensely watch him and follow him about, thereby isolating him from the patient community as a specially dangerous case; then, at the least provocation, they medicate and seclude him." Wilmer concludes: "The staff's fear . . . communicates itself to the patient. If we expect that he is going to attempt suicide, our expectation is communicated to him by the elaborate precautions we are taking. This only increases the chances he will do so."[67]

There is much ambivalence in this society regarding suicide and that ambivalence affects greatly the control process. The inevitability of death and the will to live conflict in most of us. Suicide is a way of resolving that conflict although not one that many consider sufficiently rewarding. When an individual attempts or commits suicide, others not infrequently react with envy and resentment; they are intrigued and appalled. The frustration of conflict drives aggressive responses toward the suicidal person. This helps to account for the heavy dosage of labeling directed at the self-destructive individual. When he communicates any sign of suicide, ambivalence is triggered anew in others. Without being aware that they are doing so others may, in their anger, label the individual suicidal as punishment for his action.[68]

In some societies, it has been the custom to mutilate the bodies of suicides and place them on display as a warning to others who might contemplate self-imposed death.[69] Several states in the United States consider attempted suicide to be a punishable crime. Others view or have viewed completed suicide as an unpunishable crime.[70] Certainly a considerable number of societies have viewed suicide as, under given circumstances, an altruistic endeavor to be highly rewarded.[71] We in this country while condemning suicide in the broad sense, applaud certain instances of it: suicidal missions by the military, the police, and others.

7. *The Social Uses of Suicide*

The social uses of suicide are similar in several respects to those of homicide. The suicidal act does provide the victim with a kind of identity as one who has taken control of life, who is "not afraid" to take his own life. At the same time it provides relatives, friends, and agents of control with additional dimensions of identity as survivors and as persons who may have contributed to the death. Moreover, each suicide confers additional identity upon the agents of control as altruistic protectors (or assistant protectors) of the individual against himself; they have failed in the given case, but if there were no suicide there would be no need for them.

While not as large as the homicidal control apparatus, that allocated by the society to the suicide problem is considerable indeed. Suicide prevention centers are springing up across the country.[72] The Center for Studies of Suicide Prevention is a part of the National Institute of Mental Health. The *Bulletin of Suicidology* is published by the National Clearinghouse for Mental Health Information. A not insignificant proportion of the facilities and staff time of mental hospitals is in one way or another directed to problems of the control of suicide.[73] Police officers and firemen, lay volunteers, general medical practioners, clergy, and still others are pressed into services which are at least ostensibly aimed at prevention. If success were great this burgeoning enterprise would collapse.

The suicide has the social utility of emphasizing the value of life. He marks the outer boundaries of life in the sense that short of his voluntary and violent act there exists the living world with all its rewards and frustrations. Beyond his act, as it were, there is nothing, unless it be the supernatural. Like the homicidal person, he makes possible an added measure of organization for the living that might otherwise not obtain: they draw together against death.

Others have a special opportunity to aggress against the individual who gives a sign of impending suicide. Those others can guide him toward his demise under the guise of helping him to live. When they isolate him, label him, and otherwise facilitate his death, they are not only providing themselves with identity, maintaining a growing control apparatus, and allowing for social organization; they are also venting aggression. The suicidal person himself has the opportunity to aggress against them through his self-destructive act, thereby quite often generating guilt in those others.

In Coser's terms, suicide may make possible a sense of achievement.[74] It does provide the victim with a solution to his difficulties. And it may give agents of control a sense of achievement even though they have in the given case not been successful. They have tried, they have done their "best" and as they are wont to proclaim, they "learn by making mistakes."

Suicide can serve as a danger signal that severe difficulties exist at certain points in the society, that either tension is low or that it decreases abruptly at those points. Thus skid roads, black ghettos, and retirement villages are the sites of much suicide by males.[75] The process of social loss—loss of prestige, income, occupation—that is involved in the suicidal outcome and that is due in part at least to excessive competition is in itself a danger. Rashes of suicides in various types of institutions—prisons, hospitals, schools, the military—serve as signals of impending disaster. An excellent case study of this is Kobler and Stotland's account of a series of suicides in a mental hospital, a series intertwined with the hospital's gradual disintegration.[76]

Relatedly, high incidences of suicide may have a catalytic effect in regard to inducing social change.[77] There are often official investigations of institutions—hospitals, prisons, schools—that show especially high suicide rates. There is some concern in this society about the sterile qualities of retirement.[78] National programs to involve the elderly in the reduction of social ills of various kinds exemplify this concern.

8. *Some Effective Controls*

As with homicide, then, the social control process leaves the problem of suicidal behavior largely undisturbed. Much might be done although perhaps at the not inconsiderable cost of at least some of the social uses just enumerated. Within the theoretical framework here developed, the most likely condition for suicide would seem to be low tension levels in both individuals' inner status and role systems and the social systems in which they participate. Those levels of tension in the inner system may be the result of a sustained perceived lack of interference among performances or of sudden and large decreases in perceived interference. Low tension in the social system may be a consequence of a prolonged condition of high reciprocity in role relationships or of an abrupt and large increase in reciprocity. In any of these cases, the effective control of suicide will depend on increasing tension in both the inner systems of individuals and in those social systems that constitute their environments.

At the same time, attempts to exert effective control must be carried out with great care or much harm can result. As has been indicated, well-intentioned help for the suicidal person often means that tension in his inner system and in the social systems surrounding him is reduced still further and his chances for avoiding suicide worsened. There must be a careful judgment as to whether tension is beginning to increase without the efforts of agents of social control. If so, then it will be well if those agents do nothing.[79] If they take actions that increase tension when it is already on the rise, then they may precipitate a reaction-formation to low tension conditions.

In any case, it will be wise for agents of control—whether formal agents or highly informal agents such as family members —to avoid labeling of persons, children or adults, as suicidal. There is in the society an expectation that those who suffer losses of various sorts will become depressed. This often sets the scene for labeling as "potentially suicidal." The overriding necessity in the case of a person who suffers loss, experiences depression and gives signs of suicide is to involve him in interpersonal enterprises, situations where tension is not low, preferably is moderate, and label him as having the will to live rather than the will to die. He must not be watched. Rather, he must be involved. Thus will his identity be nourished. Thus will he be seen and come to see himself as a person with a future.

For example, individuals in mental hospitals who have given signs of suicide can often be put to work in wards where there is considerable turmoil and a shortage of trained personnel. While he may well not say so, the person who has contemplated suicide is likely to welcome this type of environment and to thrive in it. In mental hospitals and elsewhere, if opportunity structures are changed such that individuals who have been experiencing low tension are provided with alternates to that low tension, they will often grasp them readily.[80]

Conditions that contribute to social losses of various kinds as well as to conditions that maintain low tension need to be modified if suicide is to decrease in the society at large. What this really means is that points of very severe unreciprocity and competition and points of great reciprocity and cooperation must both be changed such that they are less extreme.[81] It is excessive competition that in many respects generates loss, especially loss of jobs and prestige. Therefore, if suicide is to be reduced, one of many necessities will be to reduce the likelihood that individuals will lose their jobs or be bypassed in promotions and so become downwardly mobile. Regarding those who nonetheless do become downwardly mobile, it will be well to render less available "refuges" of low tension such as skid road areas.

Regarding the last point, to the extent that institutionalized social systems of a retreatist nature exist,[82] efforts should be made to modify them but not to eliminate them entirely. Those efforts should in most instances be sufficient in themselves to accomplish the task. For participants in retreatist systems in low tension will take arms against those who would change them and in the process raise tension. (In some instances where neighborhoods have been threatened by total destruction because of urban renewal programs and have resisted successfully, these participants have gained "a new lease on life."[83]) If on the other hand, action against those systems were overly strong and they were eliminated, then very likely participants would not themselves be changed but would simply gravitate to other social systems in low tension.

Action taken can of course lead to overcontrol, to shifts in social systems from low to high tension, even if reaction-formation is not involved. However, if this is not the case and if low tension in social systems is raised somewhat, then it can be expected that delusion will decrease. Delusion is at basis very nearly a last-ditch defense against extremes of tension in the social environment, against over- or underreciprocity. Other things equal, once the pressure of demand for it has passed, delusion will disappear.

At the same time and whether the concern is with delusion or otherwise, the past life history of the individual plays of course a significant part in determining present behavior. While situational context is an extremely important determinant of behavior, it is far from all-dominant.[84] By illustration, persons who have experienced much low tension in their social environment in early life, who have thus developed inner systems in low tension and have become delusionary, will not necessarily be changed because tension is increased in the situations in which they have moved. This may be simply because those individuals will tend to seek out and participate in new situations that are similar to those in which they took part in earlier life.[85]

As just indicated, if tension were increased to a moderate level in all low tension situations in a society (and if tension were reduced to middle-range in those situations in high tension), then delusion would cease. But such is hardly likely to be the case. The simple point can hardly be overstressed: Individuals and situations have an affinity for each other that tends to re-create whatever obtained in childhood. Participants in given situations must be persons who know from past experience how to operate in them if those situations are to continue to exist. The individual tends to need situations similar to those of his childhood however frustrating those situations may have been. For he did survive in those situations and so they have come through association to stand for life itself.[86]

Finally, humans tend toward extremes. It is by extremes that they define life.[87] The middle ground is ambiguous and anxiety-provoking for many. How to obviate this set of conditions is a central problem in human affairs. Men have been reared in an environment of extremes and so they find the unknown that lies between those extremes especially fearful. That is, the problem is in part simply one of tradition, of what has been usual. In a very real and often ignored sense, it is to that problem that mass violent disorders speak. This is the concern of the pages ahead.

PART III:

MASS VIOLENCE:
RACE RIOTS

CHAPTER VIII

Race Riots, the Social System, and the Individual

1. *The Nature of Collective Behavior*

In turning to considerations of mass violence in the United States and of racial riots in particular, the first necessity is to summarize various of the ways in which the general idea of collective behavior has been construed and to review several theoretical approaches to such behavior. Collective behavior has in the main been seen as anti-social and deviant activity on a mass scale.

LeBon spoke of "unconscious and brutal crowds known, justifiably enough, as barbarians. Civilizations as yet have only been created and directed by a small intellectual aristocracy, never by crowds. Crowds are powerful only for destruction. Their rule is always tantamount to a barbarian phase. A civilization involves fixed rules, discipline, a passing from the instinctive to the rational state, forethought for the future, an elevated degree of culture—all of them conditions that crowds, left to themselves, have invariably shown themselves incapable of realizing."[1]

Turner and Killian write: " 'Collectivity' can be used to refer to that kind of group characterized by the spontaneous development of norms and organization which contradict or reinterpret the norms and organization of the society. Collective behavior is the study of the behavior of collectivities."[2] Blumer holds that collective behavior refers to participants in a large group behaving together where their behavior does not follow cultural prescription. A crowd, a form of collective behavior, is for Blumer latent with destructive and constructive possibilities.[3]

Smelser views collective behavior as made up of collective outbursts and movements of several main types: panics; crazes; hostile outbursts; norm-oriented movements, often of a religious nature. For Smelser, collective behavior is mass behavior that is

151

not institutionalized. "The defining characteristic (of collective behavior is) the kind of (generalized) belief under which behavior is mobilized."[4]

Skolnick points to a widespread and fundamental flaw in most formulations of collective behavior.[5] That mass behavior which is not aligned with the values of the *status quo* has generally been labeled by both political officials and behavioral scientists as non-institutionalized and hence irrational, maladjustive and "likely to be foolish, disgusting or evil."[6] In contrast, other behavior, "normal" behavior, is seen as rational and adjustive. "Normal" behavior may in fact contain as large components of the irrational and the aggressive as collective behavior. And collective behavior may be no less normal, no more abnormal than other behavior. But viewed from the standpoint of established power groups, riots are irrational and abnormal for they threaten the existence of those groups. And sociologists and social psychologists have tended, without necessarily any conscious attempt at collusion, to interpret riots from the same vantage point.

What has been overlooked, Skolnick suggests, is the political character of riots and other collective behavior.[7] Because individuals who riot have aims that are quite different from those in power their behavior has been categorized as unpatterned and bizarre. Yet in fact black protest riots for example may become as patterned, as institutionalized, as, say, the behavior of a football crowd whose participants tear down the goalposts at game's end.

2. *Rioting Defined*

Riotous behavior is seen here as physical or psychological aggression toward others consciously carried out by relatively large numbers of individuals acting more or less in concert with one another.[8] Psychological aggression has to do with frustration inflicted through damage to material and non-material things which are of value to the target individuals, including their identity. Burning a man's store is such; so may be calling a group of people worthless. "Relatively large numbers of individuals" means something more than two or three persons acting together. Obviously there are no intrinsic lower limits on size (nor upper ones, either, for that matter). "More or less in concert with each other" refers to the fact that while participants need not coordinate their actions carefully, some proximity in space and time and some coordination is necessary. No mention is made in this definition of institutionalization: riotous behavior may or may not be to some degrees institutionalized.

Racial and campus riots clearly fall well within the rough boundaries of the above definition. So does juvenile gang violence although the reasons here are less self-evident. Much gang violence is carried out by suddenly marauding collectivities of juveniles who do not constitute well-formed groups.[9] A lesser amount of violence is committed by adolescents acting together in patterned ways as members of cohesive gangs. More or less consciously they aggress physically and in concert against other collectivities and gangs or in some instances against single individuals.[10]

3. *Two Theories of Mass Violence*

Two major theoretical approaches to mass violence are those of Spiegel and Kluckhohn[11] and of Smelser.[12] The Spiegel-Kluckholn formulation can be summarized in this way: Violent aggression results from the frustration, due to role conflict, that exceeds a "grievance tolerance level" when other avenues for resolving that conflict are unavailable. The institutional setting must be taken into account because some contexts more than others contain both mechanisms for resolving conflict and penalties for aggression. Thus, for example, violence is more likely to occur in the familial than the occupational setting. Cultural values must also be considered because whether or not role conflict is experienced is usually dependent upon those values.

The Spiegal-Kluckholn formulation incorporates the Gurr model of civil strife. In that model the relation between conflict frustration and strife is modified by several intervening variables: the repressive capacity of law enforcement agents, the credibility of governing officials, the capacity of government to reward those who do not aggress, the success of previous outbursts, and the degree of communication among dissidents.[13]

Smelser has presented the most elaborate conceptualization of the forces that generate collective behavior in general and "hostile outbursts," as he terms them, in particular.[14] The Smelser formulation centers on the well-known concept of social structural strain. Smelser's major proposition is this: "People under strain mobilize to reconstitute the social order in the name of a generalized belief."[15] Six major variables are taken into account. These are conduciveness, strain, generalized beliefs, precipitating factors, mobilization for action, and social control. According to Smelser, all of these must be present and in a "value-added" sense if any form of collective behavior is to obtain.[16]

Smelser indicates the nature of the six variables in relation to "hostile outbursts," the latter being defined by him as "mobilization for action under a hostile belief."[17] Three major types of conduciveness obtain: First, responsible figures, leaders, do not relieve conditions of structural strain. Secondly, channels for expressing grievances are insufficient. Thirdly, communication among the aggrieved is sufficient to spread a hostile belief.

Strains may be occasioned by lack of facilities, such as communications; by deprivation due to organizational deficiencies; by normative strain; or by value strain. Generalized beliefs will be of an aggressive, hostile nature. Precipitating factors will be such that they tend to highlight for participants the above variables of conduciveness, strain, and generalized belief. Mobilization for action includes leadership, organization of the attack, and volatility and composition of the hostile crowd. Social control centers on the force that is employed to counter the incipient hostility.[18]

Let us grant that certain conducive and precipitating factors, generalized beliefs, and mobilization for action are necessary conditions for "hostile outbursts" and that social control plays a part. The central emphasis in the Smelser formulation is nonetheless on social structural strain. Looked at in the light of the Spiegel-Kluckhohn approach, strain involves role conflict that is meaningful as such, as conflict, to participants. Viewed from another perspective, that of the Mertonian goals-means schema, strain results from a divergence between institutionalized means and cultural goals.[19] Seen from the vantage point of the tension formulation outlined earlier here, strain is predominantly a matter of institutionalized unreciprocity in role relations.

4. *High Tension as a Source of Riots*

When tension in a situation or a social system mounts to a very high level and when tension in the inner status and role systems of many participants also increases to such a level, the basic conditions for a riot are present. The excessive difficulty of carrying out their roles leads to the temporary weakening of participants' identity.[20] Delusion spreads in attempts to account for increased strain and decreased identity.

Individual outward violence tends to take place when tension in a social system grows high and a few participants experience very great tension in the inner system. Mass violence occurs when large numbers of participants in such a social system experience high inner tension. Unlike instances of individual violence, rioting participants feel they have a common cause. Broadly, that cause is to right some apparent injustice which appears to be the source of the shared frustration. Aggressive action is taken against those who seem to be responsible for unreciprocity. Those targets may be persons who stand at points in the social system where tension is highest or they may be substitute figures, scapegoats. Moreover, riotous behavior is in part a random and in part a purposive attempt to hit upon both new means and new goals. While innovation may well come into play at a later point, at the outset riotous behavior tends to be exploratory in relation to solutions to new problems rather than innovative.

If there is to be riotous behavior there must be at least two groups, however vaguely formed each is, pulling in opposite directions, engaging in unreciprocity. A frustrated collectivity or group of people can not riot in a social vacuum.[21] There must be individuals who have a low tolerance for unreciprocity in role relationships. That is, they must be especially vulnerable to the frustrating effects of that unreciprocity. They may be so because over the life history they have experienced excessive unreciprocity and have been rubbed raw by it. Alternately they may have had little such experience and so have not developed sufficient defenses against unreciprocity.

There are precipitating factors in the occurrence of any type of event. Insofar as riots are concerned, there is a multitude of precipitants that serve to increase social system and situational tension to the point of explosion. A brief argument, a stone thrown, a loud noise, these are sufficient immediate precipitants.[22] When the basic conditions for riotous behavior are at hand, if some run-of-the-mill precipitant does not trigger violence, then the formal social control apparatus is likely to do so. The sheer fact of arrival of police may in itself precipitate riotous behavior. So may some specific action of police once they have arrived, such as leading dogs from a van, giving orders to onlookers, arresting a single individual, so on.

5. *Some Dimensions of Racial Rioting in the United States*

As has been documented at length elsewhere, racial mass violence in the United States is far from new.[23] Beginning early in the seventeenth century and continuing through the nineteenth century, Indians and whites in the east, midwest, west and south clashed on nearly countless occasions.[24] The Indian wars were largely of a politically riotous nature. Blacks in America have since the sixteenth century engaged in militant protest. The first blacks brought here, in 1526, revolted, killed whites, and joined the Indians.[25] Slave insurrections of the last two centuries and the race riots of Reconstruction and its aftermath are well known.[26]

The first half of the twentieth century saw some of the most bloody rioting this society has known. The East St. Louis riot of 1917, considered by many the single most violent race riot in the United States in this century, resulted in 39 blacks and nine whites dead and scores injured.[27] In the Chicago riot of 1919, 15 whites and 23 blacks were killed.[28] A number of serious race riots occurred during World War II, the most violent of which was the 1943 Detroit riot. Nine whites and 25 blacks died.[29] The pattern of those riots was clear. Given a long history of mistreatment of blacks by whites, the precipitating incident was persecution of blacks in some particularly pointed fashion such as ejection from a public facility. Blacks retaliated *en masse* directly against the whites. The whites involved saw this as a conspiracy of one type or another.[30]

Racial riots of the 1960's differed from those of previous decades in that blacks now tended to attack white property rather than white individuals. This has been interpreted by some observers as due to both improved race relations and raised expectations of blacks: There is taken to be less personal animosity between blacks and whites, yet blacks resent white economic dominancy and strike at that.[31] Certainly this is a debatable interpretation.

One alternative line of reasoning is simply that blacks perceive attacks on white property as less costly to them than assaults on white individuals. The massive retaliation by whites that often follows black attacks upon white individuals comes much less frequently in response to black damage of white property. And there is the additional gain for blacks that the smashed and burned out buildings stand for months and in some instances years as highly visible symbols of black rage that all may readily see.

Janowitz sees three stages of collective racial violence in recent decades in this country. In the early part of the century, racial clashes occurred frequently on the edges of expanding black residential areas. Whites tended to take offensive action against blacks. From World War II until the latter part of the 1960's, the pattern changed to one of large-scale rioting within the black community. Often precipitated by some action of authorities, violence tended to be between blacks and agents of social control. Usually looting on a considerable scale took place. In the last years of the 1960-69 decade, this commodity-oriented rioting appeared to be gradually giving way to a more organized form of violence by guerrilla-like bands of blacks with more or less explicit ideological positions.[32] At this writing the commodity-oriented form is more prevalent than the guerrilla and will be treated here at length. At a later point some special attention is given to the latter, to the paramilitary, semi-organized black revolt.

The Kerner Commission (National Advisory Commission on Civil Disorders) identified 164 racial disorders in 128 cities during 1967. Thirty-five per cent occurred in eastern states and 36 per cent in midwestern states.[33] The Commission found that at least 83 deaths were brought about by the riots of that year and 1897 persons were injured.[34] About 10 per cent of those killed and 38 per cent of those injured were public officials, including police. The "overwhelming majority" of civilians killed or injured were black. As one indicator of the extent of damage, in the Newark, 1967, riot alone, 1029 retail business establishments affecting 4492 employees were damaged. These were generally white-owned stores against whom neighborhood blacks felt strong grievances.[35]

The Lemberg Center for the Study of Violence has analyzed those riots in the United States seemingly arising from racial tension during 1967 and the first four months of 1968.[36] During all of 1967, 233 disorders were recorded. For the first four months of 1968, a larger number, 251, were found to have occurred.[37] (See Table 22.) During the January through April period of 1967 but 10 disorders were listed as compared to the figure of 251 for the same period of 1968. April, 1968, saw 33 times as many disorders as April, 1967.

Martin Luther King was assassinated on April 4, 1968. Over the six-day period from then until April 9, the day of King's funeral, there occurred 84 per cent of the disorders of that month. (Fifty-seven took place on April 5 alone.) The Lemberg Center concludes that while racial disorders were on the upswing during the first months of 1968, King's assassination had a widespread precipitating effect.

Table 23 shows various characteristics of the disorders for all of 1967 and for April, 1968. They occurred in 168 cities and 35 states (including Washington, D.C.) in 1967 and in 172 cities and 37 states in April of 1968. Eighty-two persons were killed

TABLE 22—*Civil Disorders in the United States,*
January, 1967 through April, 1968

	Jan.	Feb.	Mar.	Apr.	May	June
1967	3	0	1	6	11	18
1968	6	21	22	202		

	July	Aug.	Sept.	Oct.	Nov.	Dec.
1967	112	33	17	15	12	5

Total for first four months of 1968 = 251
Total for 12 months of 1967 = 233

From the Lemberg Center for the Study of Violence, Brandeis University, *Riot Data Review* (Aug., 1968), No. 2, p. 61.

TABLE 23—*Characteristics of Racial Disorders in the
United States for 1967 and for April, 1968*

	Year 1967	April 1968
Number Disorders	233	202
Cities	168	172
Cities with more than one Disorder	39	22
States (+ Wash. D.C.)	34	36
Arrests	18,800	27,000
Injured	3,400	3,500
Killed	82	43
Property Damage	$69,000,000	$58,000,000

Adapted from: Lemberg Center for the Study of Violence, Brandeis University, *Riot Data Review* (Aug. 1968), No. 2, p. 60.

and 3400 injured over the year 1967 and 43 killed and 3500 injured during the following April. Property damage was estimated at $69,000,000 for the year and at $58,000,000 for April alone. There were 18,800 arrests in 1967 and 27,000 in April of 1968.[38]

It is of interest to note that the Lemberg Center found a definite concentration of racial disorders in, or in explicit connection with, schools. For 1967, 17 per cent involved schools. This increased during the first four months of 1968, the percentage then being 44. The Center draws these tentative conclusions: "Unrest in the schools appears to be a general and long-range phenomenon, the sources of which might be sought in any or all of the following areas: the search for excitement and action by youth, specific grievances directed at the quality of education and school facilities and rising antagonism between white and black students."[39]

The lower schools are becoming major seats of protest. While the colleges and universities have been the scenes of many social disorders in recent years, it is very likely the elementary and high schools that are the coming sites, the potential catalyzing grounds, of mass violence. Increases in the numbers of incidents of social disorder in the lower schools in very recent times are clearly evident as the Lemberg Center survey and numerous other analyses show.[40] It is in those schools rather than in the colleges and universities, that the "gut issue" of unequal opportunity is laid bare for both poor blacks and whites. College is not among the aspirations poor blacks and poor whites generally hold for their offspring. But there is for them the unmistakable conclusion that failure of their children to complete all or most of high school means permanent consignment to the ranks of the dispossessed.

6. Social Characteristics of Rioters

Race riots in recent times in the United States have occurred predominantly in black areas of northern and midwestern cities.[41] A considerable proportion of residents are involved either directly or tangentially. Findings regarding the Detroit, 1967, riot are typical: 11 per cent of residents said they actively participated in the riot and 20 to 25 per cent said they were bystanders. Sixteen per cent indicated that they were counterrioters attempting to "cool" the situation. The remaining approximate 50 per cent reported they had not participated in any way.[42] Moreover, rioters tended to be northern blacks rather than southern blacks who migrated northward. In the 1967 Detroit and Newark riots, for example, 74 per cent of participants were reared in the north. Of the uninvolved in Detroit, 36 per cent were brought up in the north; the comparable figure for the Newark riot was 52 per cent.[43]

Rioters, both black and white, are likely to be young males either in late adolescence or early adulthood.[44] In the 1967 riots generally, 53 per cent of arrestees were between the ages of 15 and 24, and 81 per cent were between 15 and 35.[45] Analysis of the Newark riot of that year showed that among black males, age 15 to 35 who were residents of the area where the disorder took place, 45 per cent engaged in riotous behavior.[46]

The Kerner Commission found that the typical rioter in 1967 was a black, unmarried, young adult male who had been a lifelong resident of the area where the riot occurred.[47] At the same time females formed a far from insignificant minority. Thirty-nine per cent of the rioters were females, mostly young adults and almost all blacks.[48] Regardless of sex, 56 per cent of the rioters were single as compared to 50 per cent of uninvolved residents. It is of interest that there were proportionately over twice as many divorced or separated persons among the rioters as among the non-rioters; the percentages, respectively, were 14 and six.[49]

Socio-economically, rioters tend to be a cross-section of the lower-class community. To be sure, some are very poor and some are modestly well-to-do. However, in a study of rioters across the country in 1967, Fogelson and Hill found that three-quarters of those arrested were employed and between half and three-quarters were employed in semi-skilled or skilled occupations.[50] Again, referring to the report of the Kerner Commission, these findings are relevant: the typical 1967 racial rioter was economically in about the same position as was the typical resident of the riot area. However, the rioter had completed several years of high school and was thus better educated than the average resident.[51]

Such data as these refute the "riff-raff" theory of rioting, that rioters are predominantly "unemployed, criminal, congenital malcontents who seek to cause trouble."[52] And while occasionally juvenile gang members take part in riots, seldom do they precipitate them.[53] Moreover there is no evidence that racial riots in the 1960's have been the result of a conspiracy, Communist or otherwise.[54] The Kerner Commission concluded in regard to the 1967 riots: "There was no attempt to subvert the social order of the United States. Instead, most of those who attacked white authority and property seemed to be demanding fuller participation in the social order and the material benefits enjoyed by the vast majority of Americans."[55]

Put differently, racial rioters are individuals who are acutely aware of the blockage to their aspirations caused by the white power structure. They are persons who recognize that in the urban United States there is directed toward them a massive, crippling and ultimately abortive denial of reciprocity.

7. *Precipitating Factors*

The underlying, broad forces that generate racial rioting will be discussed shortly. First, regarding precipitating incidents, it can be said with assurance that these tend to be tension producing situations that symbolize basic black grievances. They involve usually two related elements. One, a violent attack upon, or a public degradation of, a black individual or group by either a white civilian or a police officer. Two, a refusal by authorities, usually police, to take immediate, appropriate legal action. Sometimes the discriminatory nature of the original attack or degradation and the official response to it are exaggerated as word of the incident spreads quickly through the black residential area.

Lieberson and Silverman in an analysis of 76 race riots in this country find that precipitants were largely criminal violations through rape, homicide, assault or police brutality.[56] Skolnick notes that police violence frequently both begins and ends race riots.[57] So also does the Kerner Commission.[58] Graham and Gurr in their staff report to the National Commission on the Causes and Prevention of Violence point out that half of the precipitating incidents involved police and half of the "final" incidents that marked the end of the riots also involved police.[59]

An important pattern in precipitation was discerned by researchers of the Kerner Commission: A succession of precipitating incidents over months or weeks generally preceded a riot and for a given riot these incidents tended to be similar. They symbolized a particular type of underlying grievance.[60] For example, such a succession of precipitants might involve disregard by police of injuries to blacks, which were incurred in the course of arrests. Again, the pattern might be one of a certain type of verbal harassment of blacks by white police officers.

Once the precipitating incident has occurred, the beginning of the riot *per se* is often marked by sporadic and then more widespread rock or bottle throwing and window breaking.[61] Race riots tend to take place on busy streets.[62] They generally begin in the early evening or at night, often on a summer day of high temperature.[63] It takes but a short time, often less than an hour, for relatively orderly conditions in a neighborhood to shift to extreme disorder.[64] If riots extend over several days, there is a pattern of increase in violent activity at night and recession of that activity during the day.[65]

Here for example is the sequence of precipitating incidents leading up to the July, 1963, Detroit race riot.[66] "June, 1967: A Negro prostitute was shot to death on her front steps. Rumors in the Negro community attributed the killing to a vice squad officer.... No arrests were made."

"June 26: A young Negro man on a picnic was shot to death while reportedly trying to protect his pregnant wife from assault by seven white youths.... Of the white youths, only one was charged. The others were released."

"July 23: ... Police raided ... a nightclub in the Negro area which served drinks after hours. Eighty persons were in the club ... attending a party for several servicemen, two of whom had recently returned from Vietnam.... As the last police cars drove away (with arrested patrons) ..., the crowd began to throw rocks."

It will be clear that the fundamental denial of reciprocity toward blacks by whites is symbolized by these precipitating events and by the formal agents of control, police, who stand so glaringly for the "law and order" which has perpetuated that denial. It is the major dimensions of reciprocity withheld that constitute the fundamental sources of riotous behavior.

The Lemberg Center for the Study of Violence likens the national situation to "parched forests" ready to go up in flames at the first spark.[67] Since it will be long before broad social changes can lessen significantly that parched condition, the Center urges that short-run action be directed toward obviating sparks that set off conflagrations. While attention should unquestionably be given to the prevention of precipitating actions, it probably verges on wishful thinking to believe that much control can be effected over millions of small incidents, any one of which can trigger a riot of large proportion.

8. *Major Social Forces Behind Racial Rioting*

It will be understood that the grievances expressed by an oppressed group will not necessarily be those variables that the behavioral scientist points to as forces that generate oppression. Those grievances, however, are of importance in their own right. And in the case of race relations in the United States, it does happen that grievances and underlying causes are not greatly at odds, although the priority assigned given variables may differ considerably.

The Kerner report identifies 12 major grievances of riotous blacks, and categorizes them into three levels of intensity:[68]

First (Highest) Level of Intensity:

1. Police practices
2. Unemployment
3. Inadequate housing

Second Level of Intensity:

4. Inadequate education
5. Poor recreational facilities
6. Ineffectiveness of the political structure

Third Level of Intensity:

7. Disrespectful white attitudes
8. Discriminatory justice
9. Inadequacy of federal programs
10. Inadequacy of municipal services
11. Discriminatory consumer practices
12. Inadequate welfare programs

Police hostility and brutality toward blacks and police discrimination against blacks in law enforcement procedures are facts and not simply questionable generalizations pieced together from a few bits and pieces of information. As Skolnick, author of *The Politics of Protest*,[69] writes: "Our review of studies of the police revealed unanimity in findings on this point: the majority of rank and file policemen are hostile toward black people."[70] While generally this is not formal policy of police departments, in some it may be such. Skolnick points out that, "in the Miami Police Department under Chief Headley, official policy may encourage anti-black actions."[71]

William Westley, a sociologist who has closely analyzed police behavior, says, "No white policemen with whom the author has had contact failed to mock the Negro, to use some type of stereotyped categorization, and to refer to interaction with the Negro in an exaggerated dialect...."[72] The United States Civil Rights Commission issued in 1961 a report, *Justice*, which documents police violence toward blacks in various parts of the country. Black and Riess conducted a direct observational study of police in Boston, Chicago, and Washington in 1966. They found that 72 per cent of police on the job expressed in their everyday behavior "extreme or considerable prejudice" toward blacks.[73]

It is common for police to speak of going out "to shoot a nigger tonight." Nightsticks and riot batons are sometimes referred to as "nigger knockers." And Skolnick points to a vivid example of police prejudice in Cleveland: "Following the July, 1968 shootout between police and black militants . . . when white police were withdrawn from the ghetto for one night to allow black community leaders to quell the rioting, racist abuse of Mayor Carl B. Stokes, a Negro, could be heard on the police radio. And posters with a picture of the Mayor under the words, 'Wanted for Murder,' hung in district stations for several weeks. . . ."[74]

As noted, police violence has been a leading precipitant of race riots in the United States in recent times.[75] And the Kerner Commission has concluded that conflict with the police was one basic reason, as opposed to precipitating factors and grievances, for black rioting.[76] Still, police behavior is in certain respects something less than fundamental in the explanation of mass racial disorders. The police and their behavior are largely symbolic of the general stance of the society in regard to race relations. They are the official social control representatives of the society's members. In the final analysis they serve at the pleasure of the society. Police discrimination in regard to blacks could hardly continue on a large scale were it not for a considerable degree of public support. Thus from this perspective it is well to avoid the pitfall of assigning an enlarged importance to the role of the police as a wellspring of racial unrest.

Other reasons set forth by the Kerner Commission for riots of a racial nature are more basic social forces. These include pervasive prejudice, discrimination and segregation toward blacks in the society at large; black in-migration to the core areas of northern cities, white exodus, and the consequent buildup of ghetto areas; frustrated hopes of blacks in the sense that small gains have been made by them while larger strides toward equality have been denied; the sheer frustration of powerlessness experienced by blacks day in and day out; a new mood of black racial pride which serves as an impetus to action; and a tacit social approval of violent methods due to terroristic activities by white members of the power structure.[77]

As indicated in chapter two, most analyses point also to the sheer frustration of black economic conditions.[78] While gains in income, occupational status and other economic factors have accrued to blacks, similar gains have been experienced by whites.[79] Thus the black is relatively little better off than he was at, say, the end of World War II.[80]

The Kerner Commission report found the following regarding those cities in which major racial disorders occurred in 1967: A larger proportion of black than of white residents were in the labor force yet blacks were twice as likely to be unemployed as whites. Black unemployment in 1967 was 8.2 per cent of the black labor force.[81] Blacks were subject to a significantly greater degree of uncertainty than were whites as to whether or not they would be able to retain their jobs if they had them. In the cities analyzed, black workers received 70 per cent the wages of white workers on the average.[82] Significantly fewer blacks than whites in the 1967 riot cities owned their own homes. Although their incomes were much below those of whites, they paid the same rents as whites. Black dwelling places were three times as likely to be overcrowded and substandard.[83]

Lieberson and Silverman analyzed 76 race riots.[84] Cities where riots occurred were compared with non-riot cities of similar size. The authors found that the differences in percentages of blacks and of whites in labor, domestic, and service occupations were less in the riot cities than in the control cities. Regarding this, Lieberson and Silverman write: "The encroachment of Negroes in the white occupational world evidently tends to increase the chances of a riot, although we must also consider the possibility that Negro militancy increases as Negroes move out of their traditional niche."[85] The study showed also that there were fewer black store-owners in riot cities than in the control cities. Riot cities had fewer black police than did the other cities. The more the local government was in communication with the average voter and responsive to his needs, the less was the likelihood of a riot. Interestingly, quality of housing conditions and rapidity of population turnover were not found to be related to whether or not riots occurred.[86]

A Harris opinion poll of 1967 shows that black and white adults have vastly different perceptions of the causes of riots.[87] Percentages of reasons spontaneously given by respondents were the following:

	White	*Black*
Outside agitation	45	10
Prejudice	16	36
Unemployment	10	29
Poverty	14	28
Black laziness	13	5
Uneducated people	11	9
Teen-agers seeking trouble	7	7
Law too lax	7	½

Skolnick summarizes racial riots in the United States as spontaneous political acts expressing enormous frustration and genuine grievance."[88] And the Kerner Commission drew the now famous conclusion: "Our nation is moving toward two societies, one black, one white—separate and unequal."[89]

The various findings above and those data on white blockages to social opportunities for blacks set forth in chapter two point to this: Unreciprocity between the two races runs disastrously high and is a predominant source of individual and mass violence. As Mattick writes, "The content of the riot is reciprocal, like a broken bargain. It consists of claims and denials made in the substance and conceptions of life, liberty and the pursuit of happiness. The parties to the bargain are the Negro community and the white majority...."[90]

9. *Black Militancy*

Both white and black militant organizations have played integral parts in this nation's development. One author categorizes white militancy as "the most violent single force in American history outside of war."[91] While there have been many white militant groups organized around the oppression of blacks, the

Ku Klux Klan has of course been the most notorious. The Klan rose in the decades following the Civil War, rose out of irrational fears of liberated blacks by highly insecure whites.[92] Loosely organized regionally and nationally and with many strong local units, the Klan has seen something of a rebirth in recent years. The Mississippi White Knights have been contemporary leaders of white violence toward blacks in the deep south. Other groups such as the National States Rights Party have also been in the forefront of present-day southern white militancy. In the north, groups of lower-middle-class whites have been organizing with the express purpose of supporting police departments that will take a "tough line" with blacks.[93]

Black nationalist groups among free blacks formed as early as the beginning of the nineteenth century.[94] The end of Reconstruction and the rise of Jim Crow launched sustained black nationalist movements. Booker T. Washington during the first part of this century advocated general black independence and in particular black economic autonomy.[95] Marcus Garvey, a Jamaican, was the leader of total black nationalism in this country in the post World War I period. A staunch advocate of "Africa for blacks only," he preached full separatism between white and black races.[96]

The Nation of Islam, established in the early 1930's with Elijah Muhammed as its leader, carried on in a general sense the thrust of Garvey's movement, advocating black social, political, economic, and religious independence. Malcolm X became the charismatic spokesman of the Nation of Islam. In 1964 Malcolm X broke with that organization and until his assassination advocated a union of oppressed peoples everywhere and the elimination of injustice through violent or peaceful means.[97]

In the 1950's and 1960's, there were these militant black groups on the one hand and the less militant followers of Martin Luther King, Jr., on the other. King's non-violent leadership of the 1955-56 bus boycott in Montgomery, Alabama, made him a national black leader. It was his aim through non-violent means to "awaken a sense of moral shame in the opponent."[98] While he may have accomplished this in some degree, the lack of large-scale gains for blacks led many to turn in the direction of forthright militancy. Some observers hold this was in part because the federal government stood by and did little to help the civil rights movement.[99]

The Kerner Commission labels militant black power of the 1960's "old wine in new bottles." The Commission suggests that black power leaders have retreated into an unreal world and unconsciously play into the hands of white racists in advocating separatism of blacks and whites.[100] Skolnick disagrees with this interpretation and suggests that the Commission's members miss the point of contemporary black power nationalism. Our history is replete with examples of minority groups who have used violence to induce social change, Skolnick holds.[101] The black power groups are following in that tradition. Skolnick writes: "It is highly unrealistic to depend on the mere goodwill of the larger society to meet black grievances."[102] Further, Skolnick believes the Kerner Commission overlooks the fact that the black protest has as its goal a transformation of American institutions rather than inclusion in them.[103]

Black self-defense groups such as the Black Panthers have come into being in recent years, Skolnick maintains, to defend themselves against white militancy by police and others.[104] Black defense is looked upon with horror by the society as a whole while white defense is a traditional right. The guiding principle, the basic definition, of the Black Panthers is that "White America . . . is holding black people in colonial bondage."[105] Unprovoked attacks by police and civilian white militants on the Panthers give substance to that belief and substantiate their need for self-defense.[106]

Actually, there has been remarkably little violence as yet by contemporary black militant groups although there has been a significant amount of violence directed against them by whites.[107] But there is some evidence that the pattern of black riots of the late 1960's is giving way to sporadic, guerilla warfare by militant blacks who are to some greater or lesser degree organized.[108] While militant groups, white as well as black, have been composed largely of male adults, there is now a strong tendency for black youths to find reward in the ideas and developing behavior patterns of black militant nationalism. Concerted protest by elementary and high school black students is increasing steadily.[109] In the recent past black student protest has come largely from the colleges and universities. It is reasonable now to expect that in the near future this will be greatly overshadowed by a more violent, a more militant, a more organized form of revolt among black students in the lower schools.

There is occurring in the United States a new phase of the process of racial unreciprocity. In the case of blacks, and unlike the past, it is the adolescents who now move to organize. For whites it is the mixture as before: lower-middle and lower-class adult white males man the barricades of white supremacy. New roles whose dominant characteristic is unreciprocity are emerging in the two groups.

10. *Black-White Interaction and Identity*

From one perspective, it is the daily interaction of whites and blacks that epitomizes the basis of black rage. The whites have more in economic and prestige terms and they oppress the blacks physically and psychologically. White police brutality toward blacks has been sufficiently documented in earlier pages. The physical brutality of white civilians toward blacks has been great. While in the northern cities this form of violence is probably at a relatively low level now, there is a deep residue of great bitterness over past physical persecution of blacks by whites, especially as it occurred in the south by Ku Klux Klan members and others.

Lynchings of blacks by whites—4000 at a highly conservative estimate—during the earlier decades of this century and the end of the nineteenth century provide an indicator of that residue.[110] As but one example of the continuing physical violation of blacks by whites: A group of Florida whites kidnaped a young black recently and with a machete beat him to "an unrecognizable pulp." The attackers were under the belief (mistaken) that the boy had had sexual relations with a white girl.[111]

There is no need to document the totally obvious fact of psychological aggression toward blacks by whites through discriminatory practices, humiliating customs, obscene "humor," and mocking. This has resulted in greatly distorted self-images by blacks, in high incidences of both outward- and inward-directed physical violence by blacks. And it has spread suspicion and fear through the total society. Whites have suffered the wide ramifications of this as have blacks. In some respects it is those whites who have actually aggressed against blacks who suffer the consequences most of all. Unchecked aggression irrevocably warps disastrously the aggressor's perceptions of the world. The totalitarian mind seems always to doom itself.[112] While few would reasonably deny that blacks in the United States have been the scapegoats in a gigantic spree of violence that has endured for several centuries, the problem is at basis simply a human rather than a black-white problem.

The white working man who is extremely prejudiced toward blacks and fears them is a highly insecure individual. As Wood has said, he "has no capital . . . his job security is far from complete . . . his tax burden is heavy . . . his national image tarnished. . . . He notes his place on the lower rungs of the economic ladder. He sees the movement of black families as a threat to his home values. . . . He sees only one destination for the minority movement—his job."[113]

The highly prejudiced white is likely to be poorly educated, middle-aged or older, a rural southerner with a low-paying job. His unprejudiced opposite number, the tolerant white, is highly educated and paid, resides in a northern city and holds a prestigious occupational position.[114] The prejudiced individual has been overly strictly reared especially regarding aggressive and sexual behavior. He tends to possess an authoritarian personality; rigid, righteous and fanatical; he is the "true believer." He externalizes his inner conflicts through the manifestation of prejudice.[115] Unduly suspicious of others, his identity is a hard, inflexible shell that cracks readily upon any sustained questioning of its validity.

The prejudiced white has himself been subjected to much frustration. In a sense he too has experienced prejudice—at the hands of more prestigious whites. He is at the bottom of the "respectables." That is, he is a member of the lowest tier of those stratified groups which accept the *status quo*. He finds it extremely difficult "to make ends meet" in the sense of fulfilling his role obligations as well as in the financial sense. As he tends to see it, on one side are whites of greater power demanding his services for small recompense; on the other side are blacks moving in to expropriate his roles. Thus he finds the performance of his roles exceedingly difficult; tension in his inner system runs high.

The black individual who has been subjected to much discrimination and other forms of oppression tends also to be extremely suspicious of the world in general and of the white world in particular. Blocked by whites from directing violence toward them, he displaces his aggression toward other blacks and toward himself. His masochism is well known.[116] The high suicide rate of young adult males in the urban ghettos has been noted. Alcoholism and drug addiction rates often reach extraordinary heights in lower-class black groups.[117] Self-injury is common.[118]

The persecuted black's identity is likely to be a split one. On the one hand he tends to see himself as the prejudiced white sees him: a second-class creature somewhere between man and the more human-like lower animals. On the other hand, he sees himself as quite the opposite: a being superior to the self-serving, hostility-laden, prejudiced white. This dual identity accounts in at least small part for the tendency of tension in the black's inner role system to oscillate between high and low extremes.[119]

The lower-class black who participates in racial riots was found by the Kerner Commission to be extremely hostile toward all groups of higher prestige.[120] His hostility toward middle-class blacks is almost as great as his hostility toward middle-class whites. He feels strongly that he and others like him have been barred from achieving a better job by white discrimination. He is exceedingly distrustful of police and of political leaders. He takes great pride in his race and in black culture generally. Thus it might be interpreted that the black rioter directs his aggression, albeit symbolically, at whites, whom he sees clearly as his frustrators, rather than at himself. He seeks an identity as a black man in the context of both his black history and a contemporary, predominantly white society.[121]

Speaking broadly, the prejudiced lower-class white and scapegoated lower-class black are both fearful of life. They are locked in a violent embrace with each other. They have come to need each other. The white seeks whatever security the existence of a scapegoat provides. The black needs at least temporarily his adversary. If that adversary were suddenly gone, a major segment of the black's social environment would be ripped away. Unfortunate as it may be in the eyes of many, aggressor and victim grow to depend on each other.[122] An inverted reciprocity develops because of the patterned unreciprocity that obtains. That is, patterned unreciprocity requires a certain degree of reciprocity if it is to become and remain patterned.

Prior to a riot in a given area, tension in the social systems of that area is exceedingly high and tension in the inner role systems of residents and other participants is also very high.[123] At this stage there is considerable ambiguity among participants as to the meanings of the situations in which they take part. And the lack of identity by participants adds a further dimension of ambiguity. Uncertainty, ambiguity, involve elements of the unknown. And the unknown is exceedingly threatening. Frustrated individuals, as are likely to be those associated with a potentially riotous area, are anxious individuals. And anxiety can be construed, as Quarantelli writes, to be an "inability to designate any object in the environment to account for the diffuse sense of foreboding or even dread the individual is experiencing."[124] Rumor spreads to make the unknown known, to bring about a precise definition of the situation.

Anxious lower-class blacks and prejudiced whites are, as noted earlier, highly suspicious. They are ready mechanisms to turn rumor into delusion. And a collective, high tension situation is fertile ground for the rapid spread of delusion. The situation that precipitates a riot may of course not in itself be delusionary. For example, a pregnant black woman may in fact be beaten by a white police officer for some alleged offense and this may trigger a riot. On the other hand, a police officer may simply have questioned legitimately a black, heavy-set woman with a shirt overhanging her skirt or slacks. And accounts of this incident may generate the false belief that the officer assaulted a pregnant woman.

People believe what they must. If blacks feel much hostility toward whites in general and white police officers in particular, then under conditions of very high situational and inner tension they will "explain" the frustration they feel and at the same time create a specific reason for taking action by generating a false belief as in the above example. Given sufficient frustration, anxiety, insecurity, fear, individuals can quickly come to believe firmly such a rumor.

Once that belief is accepted and acted upon, for participants—some black and white civilians, some police—the riot may provide an instant if temporary identity.[125] While for most any identity gained will last but briefly, for a few there may be launched a career as protester or militant. When a riot begins, for some participants there will be little that is ambiguous about it. These will be those who participate directly in the action. When one is fighting the police and looting stores in a large-scale riot, it is clear to him that a riot is occurring. Bystanders on the fringe of the riot may perceive a highly ambiguous situation. And for most participants, their roles in the situation are likely to be without great ambiguity: They are black rioters, or whites opposed to black rioters, or black counter-rioters attempting "to cool it," or white police.[126] Each is part of an acting group. Each group is set off unmistakably from the others. Participants have little uncertainty about the meaning of what they are doing. Thus the distinctive qualities of riotous situations and of major roles within them lend identity to participants.

In concluding this chapter, a theme that has run implicitly through much of the discussion should be explicated: Where whites and blacks face each other in rigid unreciprocity, there is an inevitable tightening of the inner systems of members of each group. The burdens of confrontation—both literal and figurative confrontation—drain away the energy needed for various role performances. Protagonists recognize this drain, feel great strain, interference, among their performances; hence, high inner tension. These burdens of confrontation eat away at whatever identity participants possess. Whether or not out of these kinds of situations new and non-violent identities can grow is indeed problematical.

CHAPTER IX

The Social Control of Race Riots

1. *Abortive Social Control and Predictability*

The Kerner Commission concludes that little change in black-white relations resulted from the 1967 riots.[1] Over recent decades whites have come to see black goals of equality as legitimate but do not accept black means that involve protest, even non-violent protest, militancy and violence.[2] Normal channels for social control, for effecting social change, and for the redress of grievances are in considerable part what those in power make them. As has been pointed out elsewhere, "normal channels" have been followed in the burning of witches, slavery, or extermination of minorities.[3]

The society's overall reaction to racial riots has been to tighten formal controls ostensibly designed to allay the disorders and to make available to blacks a small degree of the reforms they demand.[4] Both the increased controls and the minor reforms tend to have the opposite of the intended effect. The very modest white responses to black demands for wide-scale reform enrage many blacks. Those responses indicate to blacks that if something is being done then it could have been done before and much more could be done right now. Some repeal of unreciprocity by whites goads blacks to demand immediate full repeal.

Strong social controls of collective outbursts of discontent serve to increase hostility.[5] Police force brought to bear at the scene of a collective disorder labels the situation as a riot and so increases the likelihood of one. And that force begets the counterforce of further rebellion which necessitates a greater show of formal control. Situational unreciprocity and tension increase. Rebellious, discontent individuals then tend to organize into revolutionary guerilla groups and the force-versus-force spiral is escalated still further toward greater violence.[6]

As police apply greater force, rioters show greater resistance.

175

Each comes to expect the other to act aggressively toward the first. Thus each becomes overly ready to defend himself. In this way, prophecy becomes self-fulfilling.[7] Over months and years, discontented racial and other activists imitate the police. That is to say, they perceive that police organization is in the long run superior in effectiveness to their previous spontaneous outbursts of hostility and to rioting. In a very rough sense, they organize along the same lines as the police. Being less organized, however, they have more flexibility. Semi-organized protesters become in comparison to the police as guerilla armies are to standing military establishments of the state.[8]

In the earlier stages of protest, when unorganized rioters and police confront each other, the knot of unreciprocity in role relations is drawn tighter and tighter. Tension in the social system is raised still further as police increase the use of force and rioters resist. However, as time goes on and protesters and police encounter each other in more patterned, organized fashion, unreciprocity and tension in the social system actually decrease somewhat. The roles of police and of protesters take on aspects of those of military combatants. There must be a certain element of reciprocity between soldiers in opposing armies if they are to conduct warfare. So it is on a lesser scale between police and semi-organized racial or other activists.

There is a tendency to view the transition from disorganized to organized violent protest as socially unacceptable because it is somehow indicative of greater violence.[9] Violence may in fact grow greater in the sense that more individuals are killed or injured. However, and whether it grows greater or not, violence becomes more predictable as to under what conditions, in which situations, it will occur. Such predictability depends on a measure of reciprocity in role relationships between combatants.

2. The Police Role

In the heat of emotion, the police are sometimes viewed as paragons of law and order and defenders of the four freedoms. More often they are perceived, whether in the heat of emotion or otherwise, as corrupt, hostile, racist "law and order" fanatics, and opponents of individual freedom. Seldom are they seen as human beings. Emotion tinges analysis of the police by behavioral science. Studies of police behavior not infrequently fail to recognize for example that in some respects at least police violence is a consequence of the same general types of social structural strains (social system tension) as is violence by others.[10]

As is the case with certain other agents of formal control, such as those of the judiciary, the police role mediates between the world of conformity and the world of deviance.[11] Not all deviants can be apprehended, in part simply because there are so many of them. Yet the society makes a great display of insisting upon conformity and of demanding that deviants be punished. Attention was given earlier to the social uses of homicide and of suicide. Later, some of the uses of mass violence will be delineated.

For the present, a critical point made earlier should be reiterated: The police, and other formal agents of social control, are charged with an extraordinarily difficult task. They must see to it that deviance flourishes so that its latent social uses obtain while seeming to stamp it out. The police are, that is, supposed to conduct a societal-wide sleight-of-hand. They must make it appear that what the society's members say they want in regard to crime and its control is really what they do want. At the same time the police must insure to at least some fair degree that the society gets what its members actually desire rather than what they profess to want. To be sure, the police are far from fully successful in this endeavor. It is, however, their mission and it is at the root of much of their trouble.

The police officer is expected by the society to apprehend wrong-doers, violators of criminal law. Yet he is not given the training and equipment to do the job. Police departments are seriously understaffed and pay and prestige are generally low. Further, the police officer is expected not to take action against many who are prestigious and powerful when they violate the criminal law. On occasion he is told to arrest those whom he knows to be innocent. At the same time, if he were to arrest all of those who clearly appear to have broken the law, he would be thought mad. All of this is society's way of leading the police to carry out its members' latent wishes while seeming to carry out its manifest wishes.

A by-product, and one of some interest, is the frequent police practice at the time of a riot of arresting persons quite haphazardly and yet aggressively. That is, they arrest youthful bystanders and passers-by although there is no tangible indication whatsoever that those persons have been participating in the disorder. They beat them and otherwise direct violence toward them.[12] In so doing the police are, without being conscious of the fact, reacting to the society's insistence on doing what it really wants rather than what it professes to want: The police make arrests but many are without sufficient grounds and therefore fundamentally without legality. Put differently, beset by ambiguous and unreasonable societal demands, they abandon reason, arrest more or less indiscriminately, and vent aggression. The police are thus faced with an exceedingly complex and difficult array of demands. The fulfilling of such expectations would be a considerable challenge for highly intelligent, well educated, politically sophisticated persons with material resources in depth. For uneducated, underequipped police officers, it is a set of impossible tasks. It creates angry men who find support largely in each other.[13]

Hippy-like protestors enrage the police. They are dirty and they shout obscenities in public. They should in the police view be prosecuted to the full and in fact punished by beatings before prosecution. And then the police are in effect told by many officials and by segments of the public to handle the protesters with kid gloves. Frequently the police are told not to make arrests or to minimize the number. Often charges are dismissed against those who are arrested. Similarly, police respond to official and other entreaties to go easy on racial rioters, especially looters, with outrage. Rioting and looting are to them clear cases of serious law-violation and should be punished to the full. In a very real sense the response of some of the public to the hippy movement and to rioting and looting symbolizes the societal response to much deviance: There is the spoken view that deviance is "bad." And there is the unspoken view that not a great deal should be done about it. Vaguely, the police realize that tolerance of hippies and of rioters and looters does in fact symbolize the society's stance regarding deviance. Thus their rage increases.

The police officer meets with unreciprocity at many turns. The public does not cooperate with him. Deviants oppose him. Politicians want him to behave in ways, often quasi-legal or illegal, that benefit them. He is doing the dirty work for society and intuitively he knows it. He sees his job as extremely difficult, which it is. And he sees himself falling far short of his self-expectations that he maintain law and order.[14]

The police officer perceives much conflict between his performance in his occupational role and in his other roles, especially the familial. He works long hours, he is on emergency call a considerable amount of the time. When he goes home he is exhausted by the demands of his job. He is likely to have a tendency to seek that order and conformity at home that he cannot find in the wider society. He may be driven "to shape things up" at home. In particular, if he has sons, he may demand that they without exception toe the line of lower-middle-class morality.[15] Trying to do a near impossible job out on the beat and attempting to compensate for the world's ills by insuring conformity at home are likely to be so demanding that each draws time and energy from the other. Thereby high levels of tension are set up in the inner systems of many police officers.

Police tend to explain crime and mass violence on the basis of a number of exceedingly shaky beliefs. They hold that if there are any "bad apples in the barrel" all will spoil. Deviance however minor and legitimate such as the wearing of long hair by males or of African clothes must be rooted out, the police tend to believe, or such behavior will lead to greater and greater deviance by larger and larger groups. Police point also to lack of religion and to permissive child-rearing as further sources of racial and other protest. Finally they consider riots to be Communist plots against the United States.[16]

The delusionary tendencies implicit in these explanations result in considerable measure from the high tension conditions just enumerated. So does the recent development of militant police organizations. Police labor unions have become powerful entities. The nation-wide Fraternal Order of Police has well over 130,000 members.[17] Strikes are called for economic gain and to alter social policy.[18] At various times in the last several years, police have revolted against higher authority and refused to carry out orders of their superiors.[19] They take private action against groups they consider dangerous, such as the Black Panthers.[20] Moreover, police now possess a full-scale lobbying apparatus. They have court-watchers who observe whether or not the judiciary carries out in court the "recommendations" of police. They exercise much influence in political elections. As a striking example of political activity, they campaign while on duty for candidates in organized fashion.[21]

Because of the impossible demands made upon them, their lack of resources, and the unreciprocity they experience, police feel severely threatened. Some grow delusional. Their high tension inner systems provide at best a fragmented identity. Thus they tend to develop rigid, totalitarian beliefs and organizations.

3. *The Courts*

For many decades the judicial system in the United States has been assumed to be on the whole beyond reproach. While there have been brought to light incidents of biased judges, bribed jurors and so on, the belief that the overall judicial system is an estimably fair one has been pervasive and has gone largely unquestioned. Recent events lead to the conclusion that now some citizens are beginning to question whether or not our system of justice does in fact see that justice is done. Especially has the handling by the courts of those accused of rioting and other civil disorder brought that question to the fore. As indicated earlier tens of thousands of such persons have been arrested in recent years, sometimes several thousands within a day or two in one medium-sized city. Not infrequently they are held in detention in overcrowded filthy jails without specification of charges and denied for considerable time right to counsel.[22]

The judicial system has been woefully unprepared for these arrests on such a mass scale. There have been insufficient places of detention, insufficient personnel to process arrestees, insufficient lawyers, insufficient courts and judges. Moreover, judges have been singularly unable to recognize the political aspects of such cases, both as these concern themselves and the defendants. (What are the judges' political views as to the efficacy of riots? Do they understand that while certain riotous acts may be technically criminal, from the defendants' standpoint they are clearly political?) Many judges quite definitely prejudge these cases, feeling that allegedly taking part in a riot and the fact of a riot itself override the usual constitutional safeguards which are the rights of all of those accused.[23]

Illegally high bail is frequently set by judges in these cases. On occasion defendants are illegally denied any possibility of bail. Either amounts to preventive detention that has no basis in law. Judges may avoid informing defendants of their various rights in relation to trial, reasoning that rioters do not merit such treatment although in the law *per se* they are guaranteed it. Defendants are likely to be tongue-lashed and labeled by judges in the implicit sense of political wrongdoing: "destroyers of the very foundations of liberty"; "those who would seek to wreck, yes, to tear down, this democratic society." At the same time, a high proportion of those arrested in connection with riots are never found guilty and eventually released because of a pronounced lack of evidence.[24]

The courts dispense much injustice in the United States whether having to do with cases of rioting or otherwise.[25] The ill treatment afforded rioters is but a special and pointed form of day-in and day-out injustice.[26] The poor in general and lower-class blacks in particular have long been highly skeptical of the possibility of receiving fair treatment at the hands of the courts. They see a two-track system: The more or less educated and well-to-do receive something at least approaching justice as it is written into law and as it is expressed in our legal philosophy. The poor find themselves guilty until proved innocent, without adequate counsel, treated by the courts with a disrespectful "we know what's best for you and you're going to get it" attitude. Blacks see again and again that for parallel offenses whites are either not prosecuted or found innocent while blacks are judged guilty and meted out harsh punishments.[27]

Traditionally the criminal courts have been charged with effecting formal controls over those who engage in excessive unreciprocity. When the courts become involved in furthering that unreciprocity through discrimination against the poor and the black, then a society begins to tread on very shaky ground. For there is no longer a formal apparatus that is above the battle. Essentially the court becomes a participant in high tension situations. This leads individuals "to take the law into their own hands."

4. *The Social Uses of Rioting*

Numerous factors lead the public to view riots as in good part the handiwork of a small "riff-raff" group of malcontents sometimes acting as the tool of conspiratorial elements from outside the society. One of those factors is especially prone to be overlooked by social analysts. That factor is ignorance on the parts of most of society's members as to the nature of society itself. Most people do not have a vision of a society as a society. The sociological perspective is exceedingly difficult to come by. The members of this society tend to see a country composed of millions of persons each of whom is acting as an individual. Group process and the nature of social systems are poorly understood. Thus there is little basis on which the average citizen can conceive of riots or other forms of violence as having social functions. He is by and large blind to the types of social functions or uses now to be enumerated. If it were otherwise, then these uses would not of course be latent ones.

That mass social violence provides rioters with at least a temporary sense of identity has been noted. So does that violence confer upon police a measure of identity. When the police officer is out on the street, taking action against those who riot and loot, he has a sense of purpose, of mission, even if back at the precinct headquarters he has been cautioned to "go easy." So does rioting for however brief a period provide some added shred of identity for the individual who is not directly involved. He can look with some considerable condescension upon the "scum" who would burn down his city.

While giving some opportunity for identity, the racial riot can provide a degree of increased organization for three groups: poor urban blacks, police, and white citizens. Members of each group draw closer together in a spirit of self-defense which contains elements of offense. Blacks burn and loot with the aims of both making known their common plight and retaliating against those who have most directly, most visibly, taken advantage of them and denied them reciprocity. Whites band together against "the common enemy." Police move to the offensive in an attempt to defend their proper role, to do their duty despite heavy opposition both from blacks and from whites who are "soft on troublemakers."

Moreover, in the longer run race riots can serve in a small way to knit together the three groups just mentioned. Violent dissent can bring a realignment of roles that means some significant increase in social order. The broadening of the political framework to embrace to a degree the special interests of the dissidents can lead to a governmental umbrella sufficiently wide to accommodate all three groups in a condition of some reciprocity, of sometimes less than undue disharmony.

Two further social uses of racial rioting are those noted by Coser in regard to various form of violence and referred to earlier: as a signaling device of social ills and as a catalyst for social change. Many a citizen and political leader may be insensitive to hostile racial outbursts that gut segments of a city and leave numerous dead and wounded. There will be others, however, who find the handwriting on the charred wall fully legible.

These others will become clearly aware that such rioting is a response to high tension and long pent-up frustrations, to indignities and unsatisfied needs of many years standing. They will recognize that such rioting is the behavior of people who act out of enormous desperation. Informal citizen leaders and formal political leaders who can attune themselves to the underlying meanings of racial protest are quite naturally those most likely to initiate changes in the various social systems of the society, changes that lessen the unbearable frustrations of racial minorities.

A final social use of riots has to do with the avoidance of extremes of low tension in the society. As noted or implied at various points in the discussion, the terrors of unduly high reciprocity and low tension in social systems are very real, very great. Excessive prolonged states of low tension (or widespread and large-scale decreases in tension) mean stagnation, decay, and collapse of segments of the society.

It is important to understand that much of the time it is not because of biological determinism, sheer perversity, or sheer chance that men are at one anothers' throats. While a host of variables conduce to render high tension in social and inner systems and hence to generate violence, the near compulsive avoidance of low tension is not to be ignored. To wake up every morning and plod through a programmed day of no challenge, no win, no lose, to do this day in and day out and to wither away doing it is for many a terrible thing. Yet countless persons do this.

Often among those so trapped it is dimly perceived, unspoken even to the self, and rightly or wrongly, that to attack and to be attacked are far superior to the nothingness, the meaninglessness, of automatic reciprocity and low tension. Certainly the alternative of middle-range reciprocity and tension offers a possibility of far greater reward than either extreme. But individuals frequently find it exceedingly difficult to deal with the middle ground and intuitively judge it much easier to participate in social environments characterized by extremes and by a seeming lesser degree of ambiguity.[28]

To be engaged in combat, so to speak, is not to be alone, is not to be inert, is not to be in the process of decay. A major problem of human life is that the urge to avoid collapse, stagnation, social death and thereby physical death is often so strong that it far overshoots the mark, that in avoiding one extreme there is a violent swing to the opposite end of the continuum. Usually a countervailing force is at work, a tendency for men to avoid massive destruction at either extreme. Yet the price of violence is very high for offenders as well as for victims. Individuals who participate in violence may be prone to continue in violence or, knowing violence, they may seek to decrease its future occurrence. Whether they throw homemade or machine-made bombs, whether they fire buildings, whether they are police who exert the force of the state, whether they sit and

watch fascinated, they are marked and they will never be the
same again. They become high tension addicts.

5. *Some Preventive Measures*

There is widespread support by both blacks and whites, support by a majority of each race, for two goals: Tearing down the
black ghettos and full employment for all blacks as well as
whites, including the education necessary for employment.[29] In
a way this is not much of a start on the resolution of black-white
antagonism and the accompanying violence. It is not much of a
start when one considers the myriad widespread differences and
patterns of unreciprocity between the two races. Yet in another
way it is a great deal for these are areas of definite agreement.
They point directly at two tangible sources of frustration. And
they indicate that amidst all the bitterness on both sides over
past wrongs there is nonetheless some possibility of a meeting of
minds.

This in itself, then, is a start, however indirect, toward the
effective control of race riot violence. It is well to note, however,
that not everyone wants to go to high school and to hold a skilled
laborer or white-collar job. There are many people who find
reward in working at sheer manual-labor jobs and there will be
a place for them for some time to come. More important, while
most blacks view the present conditions of the ghettos as intolerable, it does not necessarily follow that the answer is to tear
down the ghettos. It is clear that many poor people, black and
white, are extremely uncomfortable living in those aseptic,
anonymous apartment houses that many middle-class persons
find compelling. Converting ghettos into living places that
inhabitants find pleasant is not impossible; starts have been made
here.[30]

The main problems with the ghettos from a physical standpoint
are the crowding, the poor sanitation, the extremes of heat and
cold, and the general rundown nature of the dwellings. From a
most distinctly social standpoint, major problems are the gouging
of residents by local businessmen and infiltration by organized
crime. These are all problems that need not be handled by
uprooting people by the thousands, bulldozing a neighborhood

to rubble and building high-rise places of more or less voluntary detention.

The National Advisory Commission on Civil Disorders in its final report makes a wide range of recommendations for reducing civil mass violence, especially racial violence. High priorities are given to adequate employment, educational opportunities, improvement of welfare systems, and the construction of suitable housing. Massive programs are suggested by the Commission in regard to the first and the last: Goals are set of one million new jobs in the public sector and one million in the private sector over a three-year period. In housing, the building of six million new units during a five-year period is set forth as a crucial necessity.[31]

The Commission makes also a number of recommendations as to reforms needed at local governmental levels. Here, the basic goals are four: to increase communication between ghettos and local government, to improve the ability of local government to meet the day-to-day needs of ghetto residents, to expand opportunities for political leadership in the ghettos, and to increase the accountability of public officials.[32] Specific recommendations of the Commission have to do with the establishment of Neighborhood Action Task Forces in large cities, of effective "grievance-response mechanisms," and of neighborhood city halls; and with the expansion of employment of ghetto residents in local government, of legal services for those residents, and of assistance for mayors and city councils.[33]

These are for the most party worthy goals. But reaching them is quite a different matter from setting them. What are some of the mechanisms by which progress toward some measure of rudimentary equality and the reduction of mass violence can be made? One necessity at the outset is to insure to the extent possible that the formal control apparatus is not brought into play in such a way that it precipitates racial riots. Certainly this is not a basic answer to decreasing mass violence but it is important. As pointed out here and elsewhere,[34] police not infrequently trigger a riot by arriving at the scene of some relatively small incident, altercation or otherwise, and showing a display of force. If tension is high in the area, then force is likely to be met with force.

The formal social control apparatus, police and others, is in business to do what it does. It is not likely to give up voluntarily its show of force, which is its most tangible way of attempting to validate its existence. Many a big-city mayor has called out the police at the time of some disturbance in a ghetto area with mixed feelings. He may have wished that he could adopt a wait-and-see policy. But while the citizenry was demanding action, the police were straining at the leash. With regret he sent the police in and soon had a conflagration on his hands. But he still had his job, so to speak, because he had taken "action."

It may be possible in a wide variety of circumstances to employ formal controls—police force as a primary example—most when they are ostensibly needed least.[35] Police can be sent to use force in disturbances which occur at places where, and times when, situational conditions are not especially incendiary. In a city where racial turmoil is great, it is unlikely to be so to the same degree in all black neighborhoods. Thus if small disturbances break out here and there in the city, officials may be well advised to dispatch police to those points where they can do the least harm, where there is the least chance of setting the spark that blazes into racial fire. The ever-present demands of the citizenry and the police for action will to some degree be met and relatively few negative consequences will result.

One of the reasons of course for the police show of force that can exacerbate disturbances greatly is the frustrating nature of the police role. As indicated earlier, police are expected to be all things to all men and with grievous results. Revision of the police role is an urgent requirement if controls are to be more effective in serving actually to reduce violence. Greater specialization and decentralization of police is needed. While there is movement in this direction, much more is required: Some police would deal only with the general citizenry on a public relations basis. Some would have the major responsibility of handling individual crimes of homicide, rape, burglary and the like. Others would work only on problems of mass disorders. Still others would have organized crime as their area of responsibility.[36] Auxiliary forces of non-police would direct traffic and carry on similar duties.

While they would be coordinated by an overall office, such as that of Commissioner of Police, these various units would have a high degree of autonomy and of distinctive identity. Public relations police might work directly out of the Commissioner's office. Other groups would have their own organizational structures, directors, and so on. Officers in the department concerned with civil disorders would, for example, be well trained in responding to mass disturbances with minimum force. They would not see themselves as a police officer whose duty it is to preserve law and order according to current practices regardless of circumstances. A major problem for police today is that generally speaking they do have this self-image.

If a lone man screams obscenities from the steps of city hall, police want to arrest him and to see him punished. If a thousand persons scream obscenities from the steps of city hall, police tend to want to see each one treated as that lone man. In the system outlined above, the police officer who deals with mass disturbances would see his job differently from the officer who dealt with individual violations. The former would be trained to understand that when a thousand persons shout obscenities in front of city hall there is usually a definite political motivation involved. Similarly a situation in which three men burglarize an appliance store and haul away fifty television sets involves quite a different set of behaviors with quite different meanings from one where fifty looters in the midst or aftermath of a riot carry from a store fifty television sets.

Training of police officers which is far superior to that presently found and in greater specialization would improve the officers' sense of security in their jobs. Specialization would reduce greatly conflicting expectations. All of this would lead to police officers who were less frustrated, more innovative and more effective in serving to reduce rather than increasing mass disturbances, "amateur" crime and "professional" crime.[37]

6. Further Preventive Measures

It is of some utility to decrease precipitants of mass violence, actions such as show of police force that escalate small incidents of racial aggression into larger ones. However, it is important also that those small incidents be recognized as danger signals, as possible indicators of severe underlying unreciprocity, frustration, and grievance even though such incidents do not become widespread conflagrations. While successful attempts to avoid the wildfire spread of racial disorders are important, the underlying problem of deep social unrest will only fester and later lead to still greater violence unless danger signals are perceived and acted upon. Those signals point to the necessity for vast social reforms.

The great need if racial violence on a large scale is to be avoided is to reorganize social systems such that extremes of high tension (and in some instances of low as well) are avoided. This is done most centrally by realigning roles such that there is less social distance among the "outs" and the "ins." This is the entering wedge in decreasing unreciprocity in role relations. It involves bringing dissidents partly into the "system," broadening that "system."

As has always been the case, those who have been within the system fear losing power and so resist such change. What is needed among other things is to educate those individuals to comprehend that rigid exclusion of dissidents means an inevitable loss of power for those who now possess it. There is always a circulation of individuals into and out of power roles. Resistance to this process frequently increases its tempo.

To bring dissidents into the prevailing social systems means in the main to have them take part in one way or another in those dramatic games that constitute the economic and political spheres of life. One workable way to do this is to set up organizations for the solution of social and other environmental problems, problems that have had frustrating consequences for both dissidents and upholders of the *status quo*. These organizations will involve roles for members of both groups. If this approach is to be workable, roles for dissidents must be genuine ones, not those of "tokenism." This usually means that the playing of such roles involves knowledge of the problems to be confronted, knowledge that dissidents possess more than others. Thus dissidents perceive that they are involved not because others are attempting to co-opt them but because they must be called upon if the given problems are to be resolved.

Once individuals begin to work together all is, to be sure, seldom harmonious. (Grave difficulties would result if all were harmonious.) There is uncertainty about new roles, people are somewhat suspicious of one another and the like. There is some unreciprocity and some reciprocity. On balance, however, there is a movement away from the loggerheads condition of high tension. Communication between dissidents and others about ways to overcome common problems tends to break down extreme unreciprocity.[38]

A major problem arises in getting the whole process started. If tension is very high in a social system, there is little opportunity for innovation. One approach is to rely initially on particular individuals with inner systems in moderate tension. Often they will not previously have been participants in the particular social system. Now they are injected into it for the purpose of bringing about innovations that reduce tension. They do not feel the strains of the social system as do on-going participants. They are not locked into unreciprocity as are the latter. They may be able to innovate so that tension in the social system is reduced before the system "gets to them." If they are not able to do so, then tension in their inner systems will tend to rise; they too will gradually become locked in and incapable of significant innovation in this environment.

One approach for starting the process of reducing tension in a social system depends less on particular individuals than on the introduction into that system of a certain set of roles. This is the investigating commission idea but with an added dimension. A commission is appointed by, say, the mayor of a city torn by racial strife. Half of the members are black and half white. They interact in the course of the commission's work. Members of the commission and of its staff act in something of the capacity of ombudsmen, hearing the grievances of both sides of the community. But they do this in such a way that blacks and whites are brought face to face.

For example a commission team of one black and one white individual might hear the grievances of black residents and white police in a certain neighborhood. That team would meet for several hours with black residents and with several police officers. Similar meetings would take place across the city and over several months. These meetings would serve as an entering wedge to break the spiral of unreciprocity. They would also give the Commission and thereby public officials a clearer view of how rank-and-file individuals feel about the situations in which they find themselves.

Following this initial step, blacks and whites would be organized into problem-solving groups of the type mentioned above. Much of their work would be directed toward opening up channels of access to various social roles, especially educational and occupational social roles. By and large this would mean that more blacks would be recruited into roles from which previously they had been in large measure blocked and excluded. It would mean further that in many instances standards for admission to roles would be relaxed somewhat.

Now if unreciprocity between a dominant and a less dominant group is to be decreased, then the members of the dominant group must be rewarded as must the others. But relaxing admission standards to valued roles is a change that members of dominant groups usually find highly frustrating. They have worked hard to meet exacting standards and so should others, they feel. Further, the quality of the role will necessarily be lowered, members of the dominant group hold. This threatens their identity for it is they who play the roles which will decrease in quality.

The necessity then is to lead dominant group members to see that they have more to gain than to lose by lowering admission requirements to certain roles. There is a tendency for requirements to grow more and more elaborate and demanding, thus choking off the supply of new blood. Those who already play the roles must come to see this and to understand that unless entrance criteria are relaxed the ground will eventually be cut from under them.

Roles tend to grow removed from the social uses they originally served. By way of illustration, university professors who once taught many students frequently teach few now. The role of graduate-teaching assistant has come to fill the gap to some degree. But that role is part-time and it is essentially a student role; teaching assistants are not members of faculties; and so on. Thus one of the major thrusts of student unrest has been to have young scholars part-way through their graduate study accepted as regular faculty.[39]

This has been especially so in regard to black studies programs. Blacks who otherwise would be graduate teaching assistants are frequently appointed as directors of these programs and as faculty members. In many departments, young scholars, white and black, only partly trained by previous standards, are taken on as full-fledged faculty members. What is occurring is the development of the role of full-time teacher (and administrator), filled by young persons. These persons do not do research to any appreciable degree; they spend all of their working time in teaching and closely related activities such as preparing for classes and advising students. The graduate teaching assistant role will continue much as it has in the past. So will the role of professor. The gap between professor and student is filled by the new role in which teaching is the major activity.[40]

More than is widely realized the universities and colleges have become the testing grounds for the reduction of tension between black and white in the society. It is precisely because they are social systems in moderate tension that they have become so. There is, so to speak, room to increase tension without a bloodbath. And there is some opportunity to innovate ways of resolving racial differences.

To be sure, things can and do get out of hand on the campuses. Tension sometimes reaches the explosive level. Students, professors and administrators, often unused to high tension conditions, are sometimes caught unprepared when unreciprocity abruptly increases. Overall, however, there has been relatively little severe physical violence on the campuses. And there has been a considerable amount of innovation, innovation directed toward reducing black-white tensions largely through increasing access to roles of prestige and power.

Postscript

There has been reviewed here a wide variety of theoretical approaches pertaining to violence in general, to homicide and suicide in particular, and to mass violence. Common to most, explicitly or implicitly, are the ideas of social integration and of reciprocity in the course of interaction. Broadly speaking, conditions of low social integration and unreciprocity give rise to outward-directed violence, whether on an individual basis or mass scale. High social integration and high reciprocity generate inward-directed violence, suicide in particular.

A role formulation of social life has been developed, one that stresses, in addition to the related concepts of status and role, situation, social system, reciprocity, and unreciprocity. The formulation has been extended to embrace to some degree the internalization by the individual of statuses and roles; and to take into account some relationships between the individual and social system.

The formulation has been tested in a tentative way by drawing upon data about homicide, suicide, and racial rioting from a considerable number of published sources. Homicide is seen to arise in social settings where unreciprocity in role relationships is great and social integration is minimal. The homicidal individual is one who, because of that unreciprocity and because of other reasons earlier delineated, experiences great frustration in early life and in later life as well. He has had few adequate role models after whom to fashion his behavior. He has been denied access to a wide range of opportunity structures. His identity is precariously weak and he is from time to time delusional.

Suicide tends to be a consequence of either high reciprocity or an absence of unreciprocity and often of high social integration as well. There is a special tendency for social losses of various kinds to generate suicide. In particular suicidal individuals have experienced much loss of roles over the course of their lives. They too possess weakly formed identities and are from time to time delusional. Suicide occurs usually in low tension situations

193

and social systems characterized either by much reciprocity or by a relative absence of either reciprocity or unreciprocity.

Racial riots result from institutionalized unreciprocity on a massive scale. While this manifests itself in the forms of unemployment, lack of education, poor housing for blacks, it is the denial of reciprocity to blacks by whites during everyday interaction that is at the root of the matter. It is a series of small incidents symbolizing this pervasive unreciprocity which precipitate racial riots. Rioting is a political response to a social impasse. Yet it is seldom perceived as such by the wider society.

The social controls of homicide, suicide, and riots have a strikingly similar characteristic: Frequently they exacerbate the problem they are designed to ameliorate. Those children who later become homicidal offenders are given to sudden aggressive outbursts as children and are as a consequent labeled peculiar. They are difficult children and informal controls brought to bear upon them by parents and others involve unreciprocity, thus increasing the forces that later generate homicide. Further, the control process so operates that the offender takes on a life-long identity and notoriety as murdered. This becomes a goal for others.

The individual who experiences much loss and who gives signs of suicide is frequently placed in a quiet, low tension situation designed so that interaction between others and him is highly reciprocating. He needs the challenges of give-and-take, of some unreciprocity and he receives the suicide-inducing stagnation of excessive reciprocity.

Racial rioting is frequently triggered by agents of control, police in particular. Through enforcing or overenforcing the law, control agents may bring high tension in a neighborhood to the point of explosion. This may take the form of a series of related incidents over weeks or months or it may involve but a single incident.

It is hardly surprising that social controls often operate to increase rather than decrease violence. As has been discussed at some length violence has its social uses. And as long as those uses obtain, controls will of necessity be to some considerable degree abortive in terms of the manifest aim of the prevention of violence. One of those social uses is in fact the maintenance of a large control apparatus which supplies work for a not insignificant portion of the society's members. If agents of social control are effective, then they are out of a job. Other uses such as providing one means of social organization are not likely to be overridden by the social control process unless an adequate alternative to violence comes into being; that is, unless a substitute way is developed for bringing about whatever degree of organization violence now makes possible.

The pervasive and important matter of the almost phobic avoidance of low tension situations—situations of high reciprocity—has been touched upon several times. Certainly this appears to be a common phenomenon in the United States and other Western countries. Outward violence is one of its consequences. The compulsive swing away from excessive reciprocity creates situations of much unreciprocity and so lays the foundation for explosive violence toward others.

We are not a preventive society. We spend much time and energy attempting to patch up individuals who are the end result of widespread misfirings of the social system. We try to convert the drug addict into a non-addict. We dry out the alcoholic. We try to insure that the homicidal offender will not be dangerous. We do little or nothing about the social assembly lines which "manufacture" individuals with social problem behavior at an accelerating rate.

As emphasized, if violence is to be decreased functional alternatives to it must be institutionalized. Ways of doing this and of providing effective social control mechanisms once that has been done have to some extent been explored in the chapters above. A full-scale analysis of the prevention of violence requires separate treatment.

Notes

Notes to Chapter One

1. Based on a criminal homicide rate of 1.5 per 100,000 population per year and a suicide rate of 11.0 per 100,000 per year.

2. Hugh Davis Graham and Ted Robert Gurr, *Violence in America* (New York: New American Library, 1969), Parts I, VI and VII.

3. For example, Quincy Wright, *A Study of War* (Chicago: The University of Chicago Press, 1942).

4. Graham and Gurr, *op. cit.*

5. *Ibid.*

6. *Ibid.*, p. 775.

7. See annual issues of *Uniform Crime Reports* (Washington, D.C.: U.S. Government Printing Office).

8. Marvin E. Wolfgang and Franco Ferracuti, *The Subculture of Violence* (New York: Barnes and Noble, 1967).

9. Sanford Labovitz, "Variation in Suicide Rates," in Jack P. Gibbs, ed., *Suicide* (New York: Harper and Row, 1968), p. 61.

10. However, homicidal offenders have low recidivism rates.

11. Stuart Palmer, "Murder and Suicide in Forty Non-Literate Societies," *Journal of Criminal Law, Criminology and Police Science* (Sept., 1965), pp. 320-24.

12. Andrew F. Henry and James F. Short, Jr., *Suicide and Homicide* (Glencoe, Ill.: The Free Press, 1954).

13. *Ibid.*, p. 17.

14. Jacqueline Straus and Murray Straus, "Suicide, Homicide, and Social Structure in Ceylon," *American Journal of Sociology*, Vol. 58 (March, 1953), pp. 461-69.

15. Arthur Lewis Wood, "Crime and Aggression in Changing Ceylon," *Transactions of the American Philosophical Society*, New Series, Vol. 51, Part 8 (Dec., 1961).

16. *Ibid.* On justice in everyday interaction, see George C. Homans, *Social Behavior: Its Elementary Forms* (New York: Harcourt, Brace and World, 1961).

17. Albert Cohen, *Delinquent Boys* (Glencoe, Ill.: The Free Press, 1954).

18. Richard A. Cloward and Lloyd E. Ohlin, *Delinquency and Opportunity* (Glencoe, Ill.: The Free Press, 1960).

19. Edwin H. Sutherland and Donald R. Cressey, *Principles of Criminology* (Chicago: Lippincott, 1960).

20. Robert K. Merton, *Social Theory and Social Structure* (Glencoe, Ill.: The Free Press, 1957).

21. Cohen, *op. cit.*

22. *Ibid.*, p. 25.

23. Cloward and Ohlin, *op. cit.*

24. Clifford R. Shaw, Henry McKay, *et al.*, *Juvenile Delinquency and Urban Areas* (Chicago: University of Chicago Press, 1942).

25. *Op. cit.*

26. Walter B. Miller, "Lower Class Culture as a Generating Milieu of Gang Delinquency," *Journal of Social Issues*, 14 (1958), pp. 5-19.

27. *Op. cit.*

28. *Ibid.*, p. 274.

29. Marvin E. Wolfgang and Franco Ferracuti, "Subculture of Violence—A Socio-Psychological Theory," in Marvin E. Wolfgang, ed., *Studies in Homicide* (New York: Harper and Row, 1967), pp. 279-80.

30. Gresham Sykes and David Matza, "Techniques of Neutralization: A Theory of Delinquency," *American Sociological Review*, 22 (Dec., 1957), pp. 664-70.

31. *Ibid.*

32. James F. Short, Jr. and Fred L. Strodtbeck, *Group Process and Gang Delinquency* (Chicago: University of Chicago Press, 1965).

33. Austin L. Porterfield *et al.*, *Crime, Suicide and Social Well-Being* (Fort Worth, Tex.: Leo Potishman Foundation, 1958).

34. Marcel Mauss, *The Gift*, trans. by Ian Cunnison (Glencoe, Ill.: The Free Press, 1954).

35. *Ibid.*

36. *Op. cit.*

37. Alvin Gouldner, "The Norm of Reciprocity," *American Sociological Review*, 25 (1960), pp. 161-77.

38. Lewis A. Coser, *Continuities in the Study of Social Conflict* (New York: The Free Press, 1967).

39. Thus the concepts of reciprocity and unreciprocity have for present purposes advantages that conflict does not have.

40. Emile Durkheim, *Suicide*, trans. by John A. Spaulding and George Simpson, edited by George Simpson (New York: The Free Press, 1966).

41. Stuart Palmer, *Deviance and Conformity* (New Haven, Conn.: College and University Press, 1970).

42. *Ibid.*

43. Irving Goffman, *Encounters* (Indianapolis, Ind.: Bobbs-Merrill, 1961).

44. Henry and Short, *op. cit.*

45. Palmer, *op. cit.*

46. *Ibid.*

Notes to Chapter Two

1. Marvin E. Wolfgang and Franco Ferracuti, *The Subculture of Violence* (New York: Barnes and Noble, 1967), pp. 275-79.

2. Personal observation.

3. Stuart Palmer, "Murder and Suicide in Forty Non-Literate Societies," *Journal of Criminal Law, Criminology and Police Science* (Sept., 1965), pp. 320-24.

4. Homicide and reciprocity were rated by three judges working independently of one another. They used eight-point scales where seven equalled the highest degree of homicide or reciprocity and zero a total absence. The ratings were summated to give a final score which was 21 at the maximum and zero at the minimum. Raw data were obtained from the Human Relations Area Files.

5. Human Relations Area Files.

6. *Ibid.*

7. *Ibid.*

8. Federal Bureau of Investigation, *Uniform Crime Reports—1970* (Washington, D.C.: U.S. Government Printing Office, 1971).

9. *Ibid.*, pp. 62-67.

10. Much as they do in highly urbanized communities in the north.

11. George Vold, "Extent and Trend of Capital Crimes in the United States," *The Annals of the American Academy of Political and Social Science (Murder and the Penalty of Death)*, 284 (Nov., 1952), pp. 1-7.

12. Federal Bureau of Investigation, *op. cit.*, 1967, p. 7.

13. For example, Noel P. Gist and Sylvia F. Fava, *Urban Society*, 5th ed. (New York: Crowell, 1964).

14. *Ibid.*

15. Cora Du Bois, "The Dominant Value Profile of American Culture," *American Anthropologist*, 57 (Dec., 1955), pp. 1232-39; Geoffrey Gorer, *The American People* (New York: W. W. Norton, 1948); Robert K. Merton, *Social Theory and Social Structure* (Glencoe, Ill.: The Free Press, 1957); Wolfgang and Ferracuti, *op. cit.*

16. Lewis A. Coser, *Continuities in the Study of Social Conflict* (New York: The Free Press, 1967); Andrew F. Henry and James F. Short, Jr., *Suicide and Homicide* (Glencoe, Ill.: The Free Press, 1954); Stuart Palmer, *A Study of Murder* (New York: Crowell, 1960); Wolfgang and Ferracuti, *op. cit.*

17. Palmer, *op. cit.*

18. See data later in this chapter.

19. Also, blacks are more often executed: Marvin E. Wolfgang, Arlene Kelly, Hans C. Nolde, "Comparison of the Executed and Commuted Among Admissions to Death Row," Norman Johnston *et al.*, eds., *The Sociology of Punishment and Correction* (New York: Wiley, 1962), pp. 63-68.

20. For example, Harold Garfinkel, "Research Note on Inter- and Intra-Racial Homicides," *Social Forces*, 27 (May, 1949), pp. 369-81.

21. Interpretation from data in such works as Wolfgang and Ferracuti, *op. cit.*

22. Computed from data in Federal Bureau of Investigation, *op. cit.*, p. 9 and p. 126.

23. A. W. Stearns, "Homicide in Massachusetts,' *The American Journal of Psychiatry*, 4 (July, 1924-August, 1925), pp. 733-34.

24. Arthur C. Meyers, Jr., *Murder and Non-Negligent Manslaughter*, unpublished manuscript cited by Marvin E. Wolfgang, *Patterns in Criminal Homicide* (Philadelphia, Pa.: University of Pennsylvania Press, 1958), p. 45.

25. *Op. cit.*, p. 33.

26. *Report of the National Advisory Commission on Civil Disorders* (New York: Bantam Books, 1968), p. 254.

27. Philip M. Hauser, "Demographic Factors in the Integration of the Negro," *Daedalus* (Fall, 1965), p. 855.

28. *Ibid.*, p. 856.

29. *Report of the National Advisory Commission on Civil Disorders*, op. cit., p. 251.

30. *Ibid.*

31. *Ibid.*, p. 252.

32. Daniel P. Moynihan, "Employment, Income, and the Ordeal of the Negro Family," *Daedalus* (Fall, 1965), pp. 748-50.

33. *Report of the National Advisory Commission on Civil Disorders*, op. cit., p. 259.

34. *Ibid.*

35. *Ibid.*, p. 270.

36. Wolfgang and Ferracuti, *op. cit.*

37. Herbert Hendin, *Black Suicide* (New York: Basic Books, 1969).

38. Meyers, *op. cit.*

39. Howard Harlan, "Five Hundred Homicides," *Journal of Criminal Law, Criminology and Police Science*, 40 (March-April, 1950), pp. 736-52.

40. J. H. Cassidy, "Personality Study of 200 Murderers," *Journal of Criminal Psychopathology*, 2 (Jan., 1941), p. 297.

41. *Op. cit.*

42. *Op. cit.*, p. 7.

43. Viscount Templewood, *The Shadow of the Gallows* (London: Victor Gollanz, 1951), pp. 132-37.

44. V. Elwin, *Maria Murder and Suicide* (London: Oxford University Press, 1943).

45. Paul Bohannan, *African Homicide and Suicide* (Princeton, N.J.: Princeton University Press, 1960).

46. Stuart Palmer, research in progress based upon data in the Human Relations Area Files.

47. Emile Durkheim, *Suicide*, trans. by John A. Spaulding and George Simpson (Glencoe, Ill.: The Free Press, 1951), pp. 341-42.

48. Mabel Elliott, *Crime in Modern Society* (New York: Harper, 1952), pp. 200-1.

49. Other variables obviously play important parts: for example, the lack of congruence of homicidal behavior with the culturally ideal female role.

50. *Op. cit.*

51. Frederick L. Hoffman, *The Homicide Problem* (Newark, N.J.: The Prudential Press, 1925), p. 23.

52. H. C. Brearley, *Homicide in the United States* (Chapel Hill, N.C.: University of North Carolina Press, 1932), pp. 78-79.

53. Palmer, *op. cit.*

54. The Woman's Liberation Movement is not simply an imitation of other groups seeking liberation. Severe role problems for the female are among the underlying sources of the movement.

55. Wolfgang and Ferracuti, *op. cit.*

56. Wolfgang, *op. cit.*

57. Palmer, *op. cit.* In some instances, societies are so small and isolated that victims and offenders are bound to know each other. Generally, however, strangers within or without the given society are abundant.

58. Wolfgang, *op. cit.*, p. 207.

59. Federal Bureau of Investigation, *Uniform Crime Reports, 1966* (Washington, D.C.: U.S. Government Printing Office, 1967), p. 6.

60. Truman Capote, *In Cold Blood* (New York: Random House, 1965).

61. The general outlines of this type of case are reported in the newspapers with much regularity.

62. A number of persons have commented to the author about the physical similarity of Sirhan and Kennedy.

63. This assumes that Oswald killed Kennedy.

64. *Op. cit.*, p. 222.

65. *Op. cit.*

66. *Op. cit.*

67. *Op. cit.*

68. Much rationalization may be involved. The offender may previously have believed that others were his frustrator. At the time of the crime, he convinces himself that the victim has been the source of frustration.

69. Palmer, *A Study of Murder*; Wolfgang, *op. cit.*; Wolfgang and Ferracuti, *op. cit.*

70. Palmer, *op. cit.*

71. This may apply also to assault, rape and robbery victims, among others.

72. Gabriel Tarde, *Penal Philosophy* (Boston: Little, Brown, 1912).

73. Hans von Hentig, *The Criminal and His Victim* (New Haven, Conn.: Yale University Press, 1948).

74. *Op. cit.*, Ch. 14.

75. Stephen Schafer, *The Victim and His Criminal* (New York: Random House, 1968).

76. *Op. cit.*

77. *Ibid.*

78. Palmer, *op. cit.*; Wolfgang, *op. cit.*; Wolfgang and Ferracuti, *op. cit.*

79. Wolfgang, *op. cit.*

80. Wolfgang and Ferracuti, *op. cit.*

81. Palmer, *op. cit.*

82. Wolfgang and Ferracuti, *op. cit.*

83. *Ibid.*

84. Alex D. Pokorney, "Human Violence: A Comparison of Homicide, Aggravated Assault, Suicide, and Attempted Suicide," *Journal of Criminal Law, Criminology, and Police Science*, 56 (Dec., 1965), pp. 488-97; Wolfgang, *op. cit.*

85. Wolfgang, *op. cit.*

86. Pokorney, *op. cit.*

87. Wolfgang and Ferracuti, *op. cit.*

88. Pokorney, *op. cit.*; Wolfgang, *op. cit.*, pp. 108, 112-13.

89. Wolfgang and Ferracuti, *op. cit.*, p. 190.

90. *Ibid.*

91. *Ibid.*

92. *Ibid.*, p. 251.

Notes to Chapter Three

1. Orville G. Brim, Jr., "Personality Development in Role-Learning," in I. Iscoe and H. W. Stevenson, eds., *Personality Development in Children* (Austin, Texas: University of Texas Press, 1960), p. 141.

2. As do situational roles, inner roles possess facets that apply vis-à-vis roles played by others.

3. Various formulations are reviewed in Bruce J. Biddle and Edwin J. Thomas, eds., *Role Theory: Concepts and Research* (New York: Wiley, 1966); and Neal Gross *et al.*, *Explorations in Role Analysis* (New York: Wiley, 1958).

4. Discussed at some length in Stuart Palmer, *Deviance and Conformity* (New Haven, Conn.: College and University Press, 1970).

5. The author has used the concept of outer role to explain how inner and situational roles are connected. *Ibid.*

6. For further discussion of sanctions see *ibid.*

7. The unreciprocity of others makes time and energy demands upon the individual that lead to difficulty of performance.

8. John L. Gillin, *The Wisconsin Prisoner* (Madison, Wisc.: University of Wisconsin Press, 1946); Manfred Guttmacher, *The Mind of the Murderer* (New York: Farrar, Straus, 1960); Stuart Palmer, *A Study of Murder* (New York: Crowell, 1960).

9. The evidence here is somewhat mixed. *Ibid.*

10. *Ibid.*

11. *Ibid.*

12. *Ibid.*

13. *Ibid.*

14. A further form of the upwardly spiraling aggression mentioned earlier.

15. *Ibid.*

16. Gillin, *op. cit.*; Guttmacher, *op. cit.*; John M. MacDonald, *The Murderer and His Victim* (Springfield, Ill.: Thomas, 1961); Marvin E. Wolfgang and Franco Ferracuti, *The Subculture of Violence* (New York: Barnes and Noble, 1967).

17. Julio Endara, "Psicodiagnostico de Rorschach y delincuencia. La representacion de la figura umana," *Archivos de Criminologia, Neuropsiquiatria y Disciplinos Conexas*, 20 (1957), pp. 547-74.

18. Glen M. Dureau *et al.*, "Etiological Factors in First-Degree Murder," *The Journal of the American Medical Association*, 168 (Nov., 1958), pp. 1755-58.

19. For example, Albert Bandura and Richard H. Walters, *Adolescent Aggression* (New York: Ronald Press, 1959).

20. John H. Cassity, "Personality Study of 200 Murderers," *Journal of Psychopathology*, 2 (Jan., 1941), pp. 296-304.

21. Ralph H. Patterson, "Psychiatric Study of Juveniles Involved in Homicide," *American Journal of Orthopsychiatry*, 13 (Jan., 1943), pp. 125-29.

22. Ralph Banay, "Homicide Among Children," *Federal Probation*, 11 (1947), p. 19.

23. *Op. cit.*, pp. 85-86.

24. Ch. 2.

25. Wolfgang and Ferracuti, *op. cit.*

26. Margaret K. Bacon, Irwin L. Child and Herbert Barry, III, "A Cross-Cultural Study of Correlates of Crime," *Journal of Abnormal and Social Psychology*, 4 (1963), pp. 291-300.

27. *Op. cit.*

28. Palmer, *op. cit.*

29. *Ibid.*

30. *Ibid.*

31. *Ibid.*

32. Palmer, *Deviance and Conformity, op. cit.*, Ch. 8.

33. *Ibid.*

34. *Ibid.* Also Andrew F. Henry and James F. Short, Jr., *Suicide and Homicide* (Glencoe, Ill.: The Free Press, 1954).

35. Erik Erikson, *Identity: Youth and Crisis* (New York: Norton, 1968), p. 19.

36. *Ibid.*, p. 20.

37. Very likely female insecurity over the sexual role runs very high as well.

38. Guttmacher, *op. cit.*

39. J. Lanzkron, "Murder and Insanity: A Survey," *American Journal of Psychiatry*, 119:8 (1963), pp. 754-58; also by Lanzkron, "Psychopathology of the Homicidal Patient," *Correctional Psychiatry and Journal of Social Therapy*, 10:3 (1946), pp. 142-54.

40. On the escalation of delusion, see Edwin M. Lemert, *Human Deviance, Social Problems, and Social Control* (Englewood Cliffs, N.J.: Prentice-Hall, 1967), Ch. 15.

41. As indicated by sporadic outbursts of aggression toward others over the life history, sadistic tendencies are of course also involved.

42. See Palmer, *A Study of Murder*, op. cit.

43. Palmer, *Deviance and Conformity*, op. cit.

44. Interview by the author.

Notes to Chapter Four

1. This is true in other areas as well: physical and mental illness, alcoholism, sexual deviancy, and so on.

2. Marvin E. Wolfgang and Franco Ferracuti, *The Subculture of Violence* (New York: Barnes and Noble, 1967), pp. 288-89.

3. Stuart Palmer, *A Study of Murder* (New York: Crowell, 1960).

4. Psychological projective tests are useful here in addition to the characteristics mentioned in the preceding paragraph. Wolfgang and Ferracuti, *op. cit.*

5. Howard Becker, *Outsiders* (New York: The Free Press, 1963); Edwin Lemert, *Human Deviance, Social Problems and Social Control* (Englewood Cliffs, N.J.: Prentice-Hall, 1967); Edwin M. Schur, *Our Criminal Society* (Englewood Cliffs, N.J.: Prentice-Hall, 1969).

6. Becker, *op. cit.*; Lemert, *op. cit.*

7. Wolfgang and Ferracuti, *op. cit.*

8. For discussion of widespread instances of this in New York City, see *The New York Times*, Oct. 11, 1970, p. 7.

9. Clarence Schrag, "Leadership Among Prison Inmates," *American Sociological Review*, 19 (Feb., 1954), pp. 37-42.

10. Conditional pardon is in practice much like parole.

11. At this writing over 500 persons are on "death rows" in the United States awaiting execution. Many have been there for several years or more, some for over ten years.

12. Solid, systematic statistical evidence is hardly abundant.

13. Footnote 12 applies.

14. *The New York Times, op. cit.*; Wolfgang and Ferracuti, *op. cit.*

15. Edwin Sutherland and Donald Cressey, *Principles of Criminology* (Philadelphia: Lippincott, 1960).

16. Discussed at length in the author's forthcoming, *The Prevention of Crime.*

17. Marvin E. Wolfgang, *Patterns in Criminal Homicide* (Philadelphia: University of Pennsylvania Press, 1958), p. 300. See also: E. P. Albredge, "Why the South Leads the Nation in Murder and Manslaughter," *The Quarterly Review*, Nashville, Tenn., 2 (April-May-June, 1942), pp. 123-34.

18. Marvin E. Wolfgang *et al.*, "Comparison of Executed and Commuted on Death Row," *Journal of Criminal Law, Criminology and Police Science*, 53 (Sept., 1962), pp. 301-11.

19. Harold Garfinkel, "Research Note on Inter- and Intra-Racial Homicides," *Social Forces*, 27 (1949), pp. 369-81.

20. Frank Hartung, *On Capital Punishment* (Detroit, Mich.: Wayne State University Department of Sociology and Anthropology, 1951); Lewis E. Lawes, *Twenty Thousand Years in Sing Sing* (New York: Long and Smith, 1932).

21. Harry Elmer Barnes and Negley Teeters, *New Horizons in Criminology* (Englewood Cliffs, N.J.: Prentice-Hall, 1959).

22. *Ibid.*

23. This generalization applies to prison experiences, not to previous records of arrest. Palmer, *A Study of Murder, op. cit.*

24. Gresham M. Sykes, *The Society of Captives* (Princeton, N.J.: Princeton University Press, 1958).

25. *Ibid.*, pp. 65-78.

26. *Ibid.*

27. *Ibid.*

28. Deaths in Arkansas in 1969 are a primary example.

29. Palmer, *A Study of Murder, op. cit.*

30. Shrag, *op. cit.*; Sykes, *op. cit.*

31. Palmer, *A Study of Murder, op. cit.*

32. *Ibid.*; Wolfgang and Ferracuti, *op. cit.*

33. Palmer, *op. cit.*

34. *Problems of the Death Penalty and Its Administration in California* (Sacramento, Calif.: Assembly Interim Committee Reports, 1957), Vol. 20, No. 3.

35. *Ibid.*

36. Sutherland and Cressey, *op. cit.*

37. The figure at any one time is in the millions.

38. Kai Erikson, *Wayward Puritans* (New York: Wiley, 1966).

39. Thorsten Sellin, *Capital Punishment* (New York: Harper and Row, 1967), p. 35.

40. Charles Duff, *A New Handbook on Hanging* (London: Melrose, 1954).

41. See end of this chapter.

42. Sellin, *op. cit.*, p. 34.

43. *Ibid.*, p. 31.

44. *Ibid.*, p. 10.

45. *Ibid.*, p. 11.

46. *Ibid.*, p. 34.

47. National Prisoner Statistics, *Executions, 1930-1965* (June, 1966), 39.

48. Sellin, *op. cit.*, p. 34.

49. Winston Churchill frequently expounded this view.

50. John M. MacDonald, *The Murderer and His Victim* (Springfield, Ill.: Thomas, 1961), p. 345.

51. *Ibid.*

52. *Ibid.*

53. Arkansas, 1969.

54. Wolfgang and Ferracuti, *op. cit.*, p. 310.

55. Volume 5, *Justice*, of report of President's Commission on Civil Rights. See also Jerome Skolnick, *Politics of Protest* (Washington, D.C.: U.S. Government Printing Office, 1969).

56. *Ibid.*

57. Lloyd W. McCorkle, "Social Structure in a Prison," *Welfare Reporter*, 8 (Dec., 1956), pp. 5-15.

58. After many years of imprisonment, the individual is likely to find upon release that it is exceedingly difficult to play the usual roles. While this may not lead him to violate the law, it will often cause acute anxiety.

59. Emile Durkheim, *The Rules of Sociological Method*, trans. by S. A. Solovay and J. H. Mueller (Glencoe, Ill.: The Free Press, 1958).

60. *Op. cit.*

61. Lewis Coser, *Continuities in the Study of Social Conflict* (New York: The Free Press, 1967), Ch. 4.

62. *Ibid.*

63. Elmer Johnson, *Crime, Correction and Society* (Homewood, Ill.: Dorsey Press, 1964), p. 455.

64. *Ibid.*, pp. 495-96.

65. Sutherland and Cressey, *op. cit.*

66. Johnson, *op. cit.*, p. 564.

67. Wolfgang and Ferracuti, *op. cit.*, p. 188.

68. Stuart Palmer, "On the Unintended Consequences of Social Control," paper presented at annual meeting of the American Sociological Association, San Francisco, 1969.

69. Stuart Palmer, *Deviance and Conformity, op. cit.*

70. Irving Spirgel, "Gang Warfare and Agency Response," in Dale

B. Harris and John A. Sample, eds., *Violence in Contemporary American Society* (University Park, Penn.: The Pennsylvania State University Press, 1969), pp. 130-43.

71. *Op. cit.*, p. 304.

72. *Ibid.*

73. Robert G. Elliott, *Agent of Death* (New York: Dutton, 1940), pp. 33-34, 54-58.

Notes to Chapter Five

1. Contrary to the view here, Douglas holds that suicides are not aggressive and that there is no evidence suicide is "normally associated with any unusual frustration." Jack Douglas, *The Social Meaning of Suicide* (Princeton, N. J.: Princeton University Press, 1967), pp. 135, 148.

2. Emile Durkheim, *Suicide*, trans. by John A. Spaulding and George Simpson (New York: Free Press, 1966).

3. Norman L. Farberow and Edwin S. Shneidman, *The Cry for Help* (New York: McGraw-Hill, 1965); Edwin S. Shneidman and Norman L. Farberow, *Clues to Suicide* (New York: McGraw-Hill, 1957).

4. Jack P. Gibbs, ed., *Suicide* (New York: Harper and Row, 1968), pp. 1-22.

5. Lewis A. Coser, *Continuities in the Study of Social Conflict* (New York: Free Press, 1967), Ch. 8.

6. See discussion in Kai Erikson, *Wayward Puritans* (New York: Wiley, 1966).

7. *Ibid.*

8. Coser, *op. cit.*

9. It is sometimes overlooked that this conflict solidifies the criminal group as well as the non-criminal group.

10. Emile Durkheim, *Rules of Sociological Method*, ed. by G. E. C. Catlin (New York: Free Press, 1950), pp. 35-36.

11. Jack P. Gibbs and Walter T. Martin, *Status Integration and Suicide* (Eugene, Ore.: University of Oregon Press, 1964).

12. See also Gibbs and Martin's discussion. *Ibid.*

13. Durkheim, *Suicide, op. cit.*

14. John Lofland, *Deviance and Identity* (Englewood Cliffs, N. J.: Prentice-Hall, 1969).

15. The formulation to be developed here does not take conditions of little reciprocity or of decreases in reciprocity to be generators of suicide.

16. *Op. cit.*

17. *Ibid.* By status Gibbs and Martin mean a social position. By role they mean the expectations attached to that position.

18. Douglas points out that individuals may not hold certain statuses simply because access to those statuses is severely limited. *Op. cit.*, pp. 86-87.

19. Elwin H. Powell, "Occupation, Status and Suicide," *American Sociological Review*, 23 (April, 1958), p. 137.

20. *Ibid.*, p. 139.

21. Jacqueline H. Straus and Murray A. Straus, "Suicide, Homicide and Social Structure in Ceylon," *American Journal of Sociology*, LVIII (1953), pp. 461-69.

22. Andrew F. Henry and James F. Short, Jr., *Suicide and Homicide* (Glencoe, Ill.: Free Press, 1954).

23. Henry and Short, *ibid.* Douglas takes the position that upper and middle class individuals may experience as many external restraints as lower class individuals; *op. cit.* See also Martin Gold, "Suicide, Homicide and the Socialization of Aggression," *American Journal of Sociology*, LXIII (1958), pp. 651-61.

24. Henry and Short, *op. cit.*, p. 18.

25. *Ibid.*

26. Not made explicit by Henry and Short.

27. Maurice Halwachs, *Les Causes du Suicide* (Paris: Alcon, 1930).

28. See also Douglas, *op. cit.*, pp. 128-29.

29. Ruth S. Cavan, *Suicide* (Chicago: University of Chicago Press, 1928).

30. Calvin F. Schmid, "Suicide in Minneapolis, 1928-1932," *American Journal of Sociology*, XXXIX (1939), pp. 30-48. Also Schmid's *Suicides in Seattle, 1914 to 1925* (Seattle: University of Washington Publications in the Social Sciences, 1928).

31. See Peter Sainsbury, *Suicide in London* (London: Chapman and Hall, 1955).

32. *Op. cit.*

33. *Op. cit.*

34. Robert E. L. Faris, *Social Disorganization* (New York: Ronald Press, 1955), p. 293.

35. Joan K. Jackson and Ralph Connor, "The Skid Road Alcoholic," *Quarterly Journal of Studies on Alcohol*, 14 (1953), 475.

36. *Ibid.*

37. Herbert Hendin, *Black Suicide* (New York: Basic Books, 1969).

38. See Faris, *op. cit.*

39. Warren Breed, "Occupational Mobility and Suicide," *American Sociological Review*, 28 (1963), pp. 179-88.

40. *Ibid.*; Sainsbury, *op. cit.*

41. Breed, *op. cit.*

42. Gold (*op. cit.*) in work somewhat related to that of Henry and Short (*op. cit.*) contends that the direction killing takes, inward or outward, is essentially a matter of the position of individuals in the

social class system rather than of mobility within that system. Upper-class persons tend to direct aggression inward and lower-class persons outward.

43. Arthur Lewis Wood, "A Socio-Structural Analysis of Murder, Suicide and Social Structure in Ceylon," *American Sociological Review*, 26 (1961), p. 752.

44. George Kelly in Farberow and Shneidman, *op. cit.*, p. 265.

45. *Ibid.*

46. *Ibid.*, p. 266.

47. Gibbs, *op. cit.*

48. *Ibid.*, p. 17.

49. *Ibid.* See also: Douglas, *op. cit.*; Ronald Maris, *Social Forces in Urban Suicide* (Homewood, Ill.: Dorsey Press, 1969); Austin L. Porterfield, "Suicide and Crime in the Social Structure of an Urban Setting: Fort Worth, 1930-50," *American Sociological Review*, 17 (1952), pp. 341-49.

50. It is centrally loss of roles to which Gibbs refers when he speaks of disruption of social relations. *Op. cit.*

51. While abrupt decreases in tension of social or inner systems may be due to other reasons, it is usual for them to be a consequence of role loss.

52. See, however, Samuel Z. Klasner, ed., *Why Men Take Chances* (New York: Doubleday, 1968).

53. Stuart Palmer, "High Social Integration and Deviance," unpublished paper.

54. Joseph W. Eaton and Robert J. Weil, *Culture and Mental Disorders* (Glencoe, Ill.: The Free Press, 1959).

55. *Ibid.*, p. 28.

56. *Ibid.*, p. 29.

57. *Ibid.*, p. 86.

58. *Ibid.*, p. 210.

59. *Op. cit.*

60. *Ibid.*

61. *Ibid.*

62. Cavan, *op. cit.*; Schmid., *op. cit.*

63. Palmer, *Deviance and Conformity*, *op. cit.*

64. Human Relations Area Files.

65. Stuart Palmer, "Murder and Suicide in Forty Non-Literate Societies," *Journal of Criminal Law, Criminology and Police Science* (Sept., 1965), pp. 320-24.

66. Unpublished research by the author employing data from Human Relations Area Files.

67. Palmer, *op. cit.*

68. *Ibid.*

69. Henry and Short, *op. cit.*

70. It may be that in some societies, those of the East especially, there is the possibility of rewarding life under low tension conditions.

Notes to Chapter Six

1. Stuart Palmer, "Murder and Suicide in Forty Non-Literate Societies," *Journal of Criminal Law, Criminology and Police Science* (Sept., 1965), pp. 320-24.

2. Three raters, using the Human Relations Area Files, made independent judgments. Each used an eight-point rating system where seven indicates a maximum suicide rate and zero indicates a rate of zero. For each society the three ratings were summated.

3. A rating system similar to that for suicide was used.

4. Suicide and homicide ratings were found also to vary positively with other forms of aggression. Palmer, *op. cit.*

5. Human Relations Area Files.

6. *Ibid.*

7. *Ibid.*

8. Arthur Lewis Wood, "Crime and Aggression in Changing Ceylon," *Transactions of the American Philosophical Society* (Dec., 1961), New Series Vol. 51, part 8.

9. Andrew F. Henry and James F. Short, Jr., *Suicide and Homicide* (Glencoe, Ill.: Free Press, 1954), p. 14.

10. Austin L. Porterfield *et al.*, *Crime, Suicide and Social Well-Being in Your State and City* (Fort Worth, Tex.: Leo Potisham Foundation, 1948).

11. Louis I. Dublin, *Suicide* (New York: Ronald Press, 1963), pp. 218-19.

12. Based on discussions with rural sociologists in upper New England.

13. Jack P. Gibbs, "Suicide" in Robert K. Merton and Richard A. Nesbit, eds., *Contemporary Social Problems* (New York: Harcourt, Brace and World, 2nd ed., 1966), p. 201.

14. Jack P. Gibbs and Walter T. Martin, *Status Integration and Suicide* (Eugene, Ore.: University of Oregon Press, 1964).

15. Calvin F. Schmid, "Suicides in Seattle, 1914-1925: An Ecological and Behavioristic Study," *University of Washington Publications in the Social Sciences*, V (Oct., 1928), pp. 1-94.

16. Porterfield, *op. cit.*

17. Peter Sainsbury, *Suicide in London* (London: Chapman and Hall, 1955).

18. Gibbs and Martin, *op. cit.*, p. 205.

19. *Ibid.*

20. It is of interest here that much innovation is the work of migrants. Are they especially likely to experience moderate reciprocity

in role relations? If so, does this help to explain their propensity for innovation?

21. Dublin, *op. cit.*

22. For the present these are for the most part unanswerable speculative questions.

23. Sanford Labovitz, "Variation in Suicide Rates," in Jack P. Gibbs, ed., *Suicide* (New York: Harper and Row, 1968), pp. 57-73.

24. Gibbs, *Suicide, op. cit.*

25. For example, failure in the university.

26. Stuart Palmer, "High Social Integration and Deviance," unpublished. Available in mimeographed form.

27. Stuart Palmer, "Characteristics of Suicide in 54 Non-Literate Societies," paper presented at Annual Meeting of American Association of Suicidology, New York, 1969.

28. Herbert Hendin, *Black Suicide* (New York: Basic Books, 1969).

29. Although some low tension environments involve considerable activity, little activity usually implies low tension situations.

30. Labovitz, *op. cit.*, p. 69.

31. *Ibid.*, p. 71.

32. *Ibid.*, p. 69.

33. Elwin H. Powell, "Occupation, Status and Suicide: Toward a Redefinition of Anomie," *American Sociological Review*, 23 (Apr., 1958), p. 135.

34. Dublin, *op. cit.*, p. 63.

35. Various researchers report a positive association between educational level and suicide. Gibbs and Martin found for 30 states a high positive correlation between suicide rates and median years of school completed by persons 25 years of age and over. When age was controlled, however, those authors found the opposite: as the level of education decreases by age groups suicide increases. *Op. cit.*, p. 209.

36. Harry Alpert, "Suicides and Homicides," *American Sociological Review*, XV (Oct., 1960), p. 673.

37. Warren Breed, "Occupational Mobility and Suicide," *American Sociological Review*, 28 (1963), pp. 179-88.

38. *Ibid.* There is a positive association between economic failure and suicide: William A. Rushing, "Individual Behavior and Suicide, in Gibbs, *op. cit.*, p. 105.

39. Labovitz, *op. cit.*; Gibbs in Merton and Nisbet, eds., *Contemporary Social Problems, op. cit.*

40. As noted earlier, suicide rates are high among downwardly mobile skid road inhabitants.

41. Herbert Hendin, "The Psychodynamics of Suicide," in Gibbs, ed., *Suicide*, pp. 133-45.

42. An example of the last is a desire on the part of the suicidal person to have his family collect insurance upon his death.

43. Palmer, *op. cit.*

44. Dublin, *op. cit.*, p. 36.

45. *Ibid.*

46. *Ibid.*, pp. 43-44.

47. Palmer, *op. cit.*

48. Alex D. Pokorney, "Human Violence: A Comparison of Homicide, Aggravated Assault, Suicide and Attempted Suicide," *Journal of Criminal Law, Criminology and Police Science,* 56 (Dec., 1965), pp. 488-97.

49. Arthur L. Kobler and Ezra Stotland, *The End of Hope* (New York: Free Press, 1964), p. 15.

50. Pokorney, *op. cit.*

51. *Ibid.*

52. Dublin, *op. cit.*, p. 57.

53. *Ibid.*, pp. 58-59.

54. Calvin F. Schmid, "Suicide in Minneapolis, Minnesota," *American Journal of Sociology,* 39 (July, 1953), p. 42.

55. *Ibid.*

56. *Op. cit.*

57. *Ibid.*

Notes to Chapter Seven

1. Unless a reaction-formation obtains.

2. This may apply more to some societies than to others.

3. Ian Gregory, "Studies of Parental Deprivation in Psychiatric Patients," *American Journal of Psychiatry,* 115 (Nov., 1958), 432-42.

4. Theodore L. Dorpat, Joan K. Jackson and Herbert S. Ripley, "Broken Homes and Attempted and Completed Suicide," *Archives of General Psychiatry,* 22 (Feb., 1965), pp. 213-16.

5. William A. Rushing, "Individual Behavior and Suicide," in Jack P. Gibbs, ed., *Suicide* (New York: Harper and Row, 1968), p. 100.

6. *Ibid.*

7. *Ibid.*

8. *Ibid.*, p. 101.

9. For example, Norman L. Farberow and Edwin S. Shneidman, eds., *The Cry for Help* (New York: McGraw-Hill, 1965), pp. 290-324.

10. Erik H. Erikson, *Identity: Youth and Crisis* (New York: Norton, 1968).

11. Kobler and Stotland, *op. cit.*, pp. 4-5; Rushing, *op. cit.*, p. 99.

12. Farberow and Shneidman, *op. cit.*, p. 13.

13. Kobler and Stotland, *op. cit.*, p. 8.

14. Rushing, *op. cit.*, p. 98.

15. For example, Jack D. Douglas, *The Social Meanings of Suicide* (Princeton, N. J.: Princeton University Press, 1967), pp. 283-85, 339.

16. Edwin M. Lemert, "Paranoia and the Dynamics of Exclusion," *Sociometry*, 25 (March, 1962), pp. 2-25.

17. Rushing, *op. cit.*, p. 102.

18. *Ibid.*, p. 104.

19. Louis I. Dublin, *Suicide* (New York: Ronald Press, 1963), p. 171.

20. Stuart Palmer, *Deviance and Conformity* (New Haven, Conn.: College and University Press, 1970).

21. *Ibid.*

22. E. H. Schmidt, *et al.*, "Evaluation of Suicide Attempts as Guide to Therapy," *Journal of the American Medical Association*, 155 (1954), pp. 549-57.

23. Rushing, *op. cit.*, p. 104.

24. *Ibid.*

25. Manfred Guttmacher, *The Mind of the Murderer* (New York: Grove Press, 1962), p. 9.

26. Marvin E. Wolfgang, *Patterns in Criminal Homicide* (Philadelphia, Pa.: University of Pennsylvania Press, 1958), p. 273.

27. Cited by Donald J. West, *Homicide Followed by Suicide* (Cambridge, Mass.: Harvard University Press, 1966), p. 70.

28. *Ibid.*, p. 2.

29. *Ibid.*

30. *Ibid.*, p. 42.

31. *Ibid.*, p. 100.

32. *Ibid.*, p. 28.

33. *Ibid.*

34. *Ibid.*, p. 29.

35. *Ibid.*

36. *Ibid.*

37. *Ibid.*, p. 36.

38. *Ibid.*, p. 34.

39. *Ibid.*, p. 35.

40. Wolfgang, *op. cit.*, p. 272.

41. *Ibid.*, p. 273.

42. *Ibid.*, p. 276.

43. *Ibid.*, p. 277.

44. *Ibid.*, p. 278.

45. *Ibid.*

46. *Ibid.*

47. West, *op. cit.*, p. 46.

48. Paul Bohannen, ed., *African Homicide and Suicide* (Princeton, N. J.: Princeton University Press, 1960), p. 117; Kobler and Stotland, *op. cit.*, pp. 10-16; Rushing, *op. cit.*, pp. 104-6.

49. Kobler and Stotland, *op. cit.*, Ch. 1.

50. A. E. Bennett, "Suggestions for Suicide Prevention," in Shneidman and Farberow, *Clues to Suicide, op. cit.*, pp. 187-93.

51. *Ibid.*

52. *Ibid.*, p. 190.

53. *Ibid.*, p. 191.

54. Edwin S. Shneidman, "Preventing Suicide," *American Journal of Nursing*, 65 (May, 1965), pp. 111-16.

55. Shneidman and Farberow, *Clues to Suicide, op. cit.*, p. 9.

56. *Ibid.*

57. Bennett, *op. cit.*, p. 192.

58. Farberow and Shneidman, *op. cit.*, p. 8.

59. *Ibid.*, p. 9.

60. *Ibid.*, p. 53.

61. Shneidman, *op. cit.*

62. Leonard M. Moss and Donald M. Hamilton, "Psychotherapy of the Suicidal Patient," in Shneidman and Farberow, *op. cit.*

63. Kobler and Stotland, *op. cit.*, Ch. 1.

64. Moss and Hamilton, *op. cit.*, p. 103.

65. *Ibid.*

66. H. A. Wilmer, *Social Psychiatry in Action* (Springfield, Ill.: Thomas, 1958).

67. *Ibid.*

68. Somewhat similarly, the individual who threatens or attempts suicide labels himself as suicidal.

69. Human Relations Area Files.

70. *Ibid.*

71. Japan.

72. See recent issues of *Bulletin of Suicidology*, National Institute of Mental Health.

73. *Ibid.*

74. Lewis E. Coser, *Continuities in the Study of Social Conflict* (New York: Free Press, 1967), Ch. 4. Coser refers, however, to outward directed violence, not to suicide.

75. Palmer, *Deviance and Conformity, op. cit.*, Ch. 8.

76. Kobler and Stotland, *op. cit.*

77. Suggested by Coser, *op. cit.*, although not in relation to suicide.

78. As any standard work in sociology is likely to discuss.

79. Stuart Palmer, "On the Unintended Consequences of Social Control," paper read at annual meeting of American Sociological Association, San Francisco, 1969.

80. Kobler and Stotland make the case strongly for effecting changes in a person's social life space. Having reviewed an array of studies of suicide, those authors write: "The data strongly suggest that suicide and preoccupation with suicide are more likely to occur in response to a new experience involving the loss of a stable role.

Suicide, then, is not made likely solely by what may objectively be expected to be an 'intolerable situation' but by a new set of circumstances which destroys the individual's entire sense of adequacy for dealing with the world as he knows and views it." *Op. cit.*, p. 13.

81. This of course would serve also to change the conditions that lead to homicide.

82. Often termed subculture.

83. Palmer, "High Social Integration and Deviance," *op. cit.*

84. Palmer, *Deviance and Conformity, op. cit.*

85. *Ibid.*

Notes to Chapter Eight

1. Gustave Le Bon, *The Crowd* (New York: Viking, Compass ed., 1960), p. 18.

2. Ralph H. Turner and Lewis M. Killian, *Collective Behavior* (Englewood Cliffs, N. J.: Prentice-Hall, 1957), p. 4.

3. Herbert Blumer, "Collective Behavior," in Joseph B. Gittler, ed., *Review of Sociology* (New York: Wiley, 1957), pp. 129-31.

4. Neil J. Smelser, *Theory of Collective Behavior* (New York: Free Press, 1963), p. 383; also pp. 2-3.

5. Jerome H. Skolnick, *The Politics of Protest* (Washington, D.C.: U. S. Government Printing Office, 1969), Ch. IX.

6. Roger Brown, Social Psychology (New York: Free Press, 1965), p. 709.

7. *Op. cit.*

8. For other definitional approaches, see Smelser, *op. cit.*, especially p. 226.

9. Lewis Yablonsky, *The Violent Gang* (New York: Macmillan, 1962).

10. They may also aggress psychologically and symbolically through, say, theft or the threat of violence.

11. *The First Two Years: Annual Report to the Board of Governors, 1968*, Lemberg Center for the Study of Violence, Brandeis University.

12. *Op. cit.*

13. Spiegel, *op. cit.*

14. *Op. cit.*

15. *Ibid.*, p. 385.

16. Value-added means the six variables always follow one another in a fixed sequence and each "adds" to those preceding.

17. *Op. cit.*, p. 226.

18. Smelser seems to believe that control will be effective in terms of its manifest function providing force is applied and agents of control do not take ideological sides beyond those required by their formal

roles as controllers. He thus does not deal in any major way with the idea that control can generate hostile outbursts. *Ibid.*, pp. 266-69.

19. Robert K. Merton, *Social Structure and Social Process* (Glencoe, Ill.: Free Press, 1957).

20. However, and as noted below, riotous behavior itself may in certain respects serve to increase the identity of participants.

21. Collectivity does not necessarily imply group cohesion.

22. Skolnick, *op. cit.*

23. Hugh D. Graham and Ted R. Gurr, *Violence in America* (New York: New American Library, 1969); Skolnick, *op. cit.*

24. *Ibid.*, p. 7.

25. *Ibid.*, p. 99.

26. *Ibid.* Also Graham and Gurr, *op. cit.*

27. Elliot M. Rudwick, *Race Riot at East St. Louis, July 2, 1917* (Carbondale, Ill.: Southern Illinois University Press, 1964).

28. Graham and Gurr, *op. cit.*, pp. 384-85.

29. *Ibid.*

30. *Ibid.*

31. *Ibid.*, p. 386.

32. Morris Janowitz, "Patterns of Collective Racial Violence," in Graham and Gurr, *ibid.*, Ch. 10. In a general way, Skolnick tends to agree: *op. cit.*, p. 129.

33. *Report of the National Advisory Commission on Civil Disorders* (New York: Bantam Books, 1968), p. 114.

34. *Ibid.*, p. 115.

35. *Ibid.*, p. 116.

36. Lemberg Center for the Study of Violence, *Riot Data Review*, Waltham, Mass.: Brandeis University (Aug., 1968), 2. For details of data collection see *Riot Data Review* (May, 1968), 1.

37. *Riot Data Review* (Aug., 1968), 2.

38. While the data by region are incomplete, it does appear that there was a tendency for disorders to occur in the northern and midwestern states.

39. *Riot Data Review* (Aug., 1968), 2: p. 75.

40. *Ibid.*

41. *Report of the National Advisory Commission on Civil Disorders, op. cit.*

42. Graham and Gurr, *op. cit.*

43. *Ibid.*

44. *Ibid.*; Skolnick, *op. cit.*

45. Graham and Gurr, *op. cit.*

46. *Ibid.*

47. *Report of the National Advisory Commission on Civil Disorders, op. cit.*, p. 128.

48. *Ibid.*, p. 130.

49. *Ibid.*

50. Skolnick, *op. cit.*, p. 111.

51. *Ibid.*, p. 128.

52. *Ibid.*, p. 111.

53. *Ibid.*

54. *Ibid.*

55. *Report of the National Advisory Commission on Civil Disorders, op. cit.*, p. 110.

56. Stanley Lieberson and Arnold R. Silverman, "The Precipitants and Underlying Conditions of Race Riots," *American Sociological Review*, 30 (Dec., 1965), pp. 887-98.

57. *Op. cit.*, p. 258.

58. *Report of the National Advisory Commission on Civil Disorders, op. cit.*

59. Graham and Gurr, *op. cit.*

60. *Report of the National Advisory Commission on Civil Disorders, op. cit.*, p. 122.

61. Graham and Gurr, *op. cit.*, p. 6.

62. *Report of the National Advisory Commission on Civil Disorders, op. cit.*, p. 123.

63. *Ibid.*

64. *Ibid.*, p. 123.

65. *Ibid.*

66. *Report of the National Advisory Commission on Civil Disorders, op. cit.*, pp. 119-20.

67. *Riot Data Review* (Aug., 1968), 2.

68. *Report of the National Advisory Commission on Civil Disorders, op. cit.*, pp. 143-44.

69. *Op. cit.*, p. 184.

70. Skolnick cites among other sources for this: Arthur Niederhoffer, *Behind the Shield: The Police in Urban Society* (New York: Doubleday, 1967).

71. Skolnick, *op. cit.*

72. William A. Westley, *The Police: A Sociological Study of Law, Custom and Morality* (unpublished doctoral dissertation, Department of Sociology, University of Chicago, 1951), p. 168.

73. Cited by Skolnick, *op. cit.*, p. 184.

74. *Ibid.*, p. 185.

75. And in earlier times as well. *Ibid.*, p. 184.

76. *Report of the National Advisory Commission on Civil Disorders, op. cit.*

77. *Ibid.*, pp. 10-11.

78. *Ibid.*, pp. 8, 13.

79. *Ibid.*

80. Skolnick, *op. cit.*, pp. 153-54.

81. *Report of the National Advisory Commission on Civil Disorders, op. cit.*, pp. 136-37, 253.

82. *Ibid.*, p. 137.

83. *Ibid.*

84. Lieberson and Silverman, *op. cit.*

85. *Ibid.*

86. *Ibid.*

87. *Newsweek*, August 21, 1967.

88. Skolnick, *op. cit.*, p. xxvi.

89. *Report of the National Advisory Commission on Civil Disorders, op. cit.*, p. 1.

90. Hans W. Mattick, "Form and Content of Recent Riots," *Midway*, IX, No. 1 (Summer, 1968), p. 18.

91. Skolnick, *op. cit.*, p. xxiii.

92. *Ibid.*, p. 164.

93. *Ibid.*, p. 171.

94. *Ibid.* Also: Graham and Gurr, *op. cit.; Report of the National Advisory Commission on Civil Disorders, op. cit.*

95. *Ibid.*

96. *Ibid.*

97. *Ibid.*

98. Skolnick, *op. cit.*, p. 101.

99. *Ibid.*

100. *Report of the National Advisory Commission on Civil Disorders, op. cit.*, pp. 234-35.

101. Skolnick, *op. cit.*, p. 120.

102. *Ibid.*

103. *Ibid.*, p. 121.

104. *Ibid.*, p. 113.

105. *Ibid.*, p. 112.

106. *Ibid.*, p. 115.

107. *Ibid.*, pp. 98, 115.

108. *Ibid.*, p. 129.

109. *Ibid.*, pp. 121-27.

110. *Ibid.*

111. *Baltimore Sun*, Sept. 18, 1968.

112. Palmer, *Deviance and Conformity, op. cit.*

113. Cited by Skolnick, *op. cit.*, p. 171.

114. *Ibid.*, p. 147.

115. *Ibid.*, Ch. 6.

116. Palmer, *op. cit.*

117. *Ibid.*

118. *Ibid.*

119. The earlier mentioned reaction-formation to extremes of tension

is no doubt a more basic determinant of wide-scale oscillations in inner tension regardless of race.

120. *Report of the National Advisory Commission on Civil Disorders, op. cit.*, p. 128.

121. He may also find a measure of identity through rioting *per se.*

122. Hans von Hentig, *The Criminal and His Victim* (New Haven, Conn.: Yale University Press, 1948).

123. Either type of tension need not be high throughout all of the period immediately preceding a riot. Tension may oscillate between high and low.

124. E. L. Quarantelli, "The Nature and Conditions of Panic," *American Journal of Sociology*, 60 (1954-1955), p. 271.

125. And for some black counter-rioters as well.

126. The role of the black police officer in the racial riot is of course more likely to be ambiguous and conflicted.

Notes to Chapter Nine

1. *Report of the National Advisory Commission on Civil Disorders* (New York: Bantam Books, 1968), p. 151.

2. Jerome Skolnick, *The Politics of Protest* (Washington, D.C.: U. S. Government Printing Office, 1969), p. 144.

3. *Ibid.*, p. 256. The making of war is a further example.

4. For related discussions see *ibid.*, pp. xxv, 13; and *Report of the National Advisory Commission on Civil Disorders, op. cit.*, p. 7.

5. Stuart Palmer, "On the Unintended Consequences of Social Control," paper presented at annual meeting of American Sociological Association, San Francisco, 1969; also Skolnick, *op. cit.*, pp. xxvi and 261.

6. *Ibid.*

7. Anthony Oberschall, "The Los Angeles Riot of August 1965," *Social Problems*, 15 (1968), pp. 322-41.

8. For related discussion see Skolnick, *op. cit.*

9. This tends to be the view taken by *Report of the National Advisory Commission on Civil Disorders.*

10. Stuart Palmer, *Deviance and Conformity* (New Haven, Conn.: College and University Press, 1970); Jerome Skolnick, *Justice Without Trial* (New York: Wiley, 1966).

11. Palmer, *op. cit.*

12. Skolnick, *Politics of Protest, op. cit.*

13. *Ibid.*, pp. 201-11.

14. Skolnick, *Justice Without Trial, op. cit.*

15. Personal observation by the author.

16. Skolnick, *Politics of Protest, op. cit.*, pp. 188-98.

17. *Ibid.*, p. 203.

18. *Ibid.*, p. 204.

19. *Ibid.*, pp. 206-8.

20. *Ibid.*

21. *Ibid.*, p. 210.

22. *Ibid.*, Ch. VIII.

23. *Ibid.*

24. This is in part because the police frequently arrest youthful bystanders and passersby at the time of a riot.

25. Skolnick, *op. cit.*

26. *Ibid.*, p. 233.

27. Harold Garfinkel, "Research Note on Inter- and Intra-Racial Homicides," *Social Forces*, 27 (May, 1949), pp. 369-81.

28. Especially is this so when individuals feel threatened.

29. Louis Harris, "After the Riots: A Survey," *Newsweek* (Aug. 21, 1967), pp. 18-19.

30. Now this beginning trend seems to be reversing itself.

31. *National Advisory Committee on Civil Disorders, op. cit.*

32. *Ibid.*, p. 288.

33. *Ibid.*, pp. 289-95.

34. Palmer, "On the Unintended Consequences of Social Control," *op. cit.*

35. *Ibid.*

36. There are other possibilities, for example, drug-abuse.

37. In the broadest sense this applies to the court: reorganization of the role of the judiciary, training for judges, and so on.

38. At the same time, the search for scapegoats and similar forms of aggression will to some degree be in evidence.

39. Student protesters are frequently unaware that this is a major goal of campus disorders.

40. Admission requirements to undergraduate and graduate schools have of course been relaxed somewhat in recent years as well as admission requirements to the teaching profession.

Index